THE *Wibbly-Wobbly, Timey-Wimey* TRIVIA QUIZ:

An Unauthorized Doctor Who *Companion*

DON J. KROUSKOP

The Wibbly-Wobbly, Timey-Wimey Trivia Quiz: An Unauthorized Doctor Who *Companion*
© 2011 Don J. Krouskop. All Rights Reserved.

No part of this book may be reproduced in any form or by any means, electronic, mechanical, digital, photocopying or recording, except for the inclusion in a review, without permission in writing from the publisher.

Published in the USA by:
BearManor Media
PO Box 1129
Duncan, Oklahoma 73534-1129
www.bearmanormedia.com

ISBN 978-1-59393-637-2

Printed in the United States of America.
Cover illustration by Beth Maurer.
Book design by Brian Pearce | Red Jacket Press.

Table of Contents

This book is dedicated to the great Nicholas Courtney (1929–2011).
Rest peacefully, dear old soldier. You've earned it.

Acknowledgements

THIS BOOK COULD NOT HAVE BEEN WRITTEN WITHOUT the tireless support and generous contributions of a number of people. I'd like to thank Norma Krouskop for her superhuman patience and unconditional love; Lewis Austin for showing me the light; Beth Maurer for going above and beyond the call of duty assisting in this endeavor; Mack Blankenship and Jocelyn Tanis for providing daily encouragement throughout the writing process; Sean Hyde and Ken Knight for their invaluable insight and advice; and Jeff Snyder and Eric and Serena Childers for all of the lovely holiday gift cards that helped fill my DVD shelves with *Doctor Who*-y goodness.

Above all, though, I'd like to express my eternal gratitude to all of the men and women who worked so hard to bring *Doctor Who* to the screen since 1963. Without these incredibly gifted and creative people, my life would be decidedly smaller on the inside than it is on the outside.

Introduction

ON SATURDAY, NOVEMBER 23, 1963, TWO LONDON SCHOOL teachers followed a peculiar student into a junkyard and began the most fantastic science-fiction adventure in television history — an adventure which continues (albeit, minus the two inquisitive educators and their unusual pupil) to this day.

In the nearly half century since *Doctor Who* premiered in the United Kingdom, millions of viewers in more than fifty countries worldwide have thrilled to the time-traveling, galaxy-hopping exploits of a quirky alien in a little blue police box. From 1963 to 1989, the Doctor and his ever-changing line-up of traveling companions were fixtures of British television. In 2005, after a sixteen-year absence, the program made a triumphant return, becoming so popular around the globe that it's already spawned three successful spin-offs. In the interim between series, the Doctor's adventures continued in an American television movie, produced by FOX. Today, *Doctor Who* is watched by more people worldwide than ever before.

Literally hundreds of books have been written about this extraordinary program, but there's never been a volume dedicated to testing the die-hard fan's knowledge of *Doctor Who*.... until now! Think you know the history of Gallifrey's most famous renegade Time Lord? Think you possess the knowledge to outwit the Daleks, the Cybermen, the Weeping Angels, or the Master? Believe you know who built K-9, where the Ice Warriors hail from, and who won the Time War? If so, *The Wibbly-Wobbly, Timey-Wimey Trivia Quiz* is for you.

In these pages, your *Doctor Who* expertise will be challenged with more than 1,000 questions, covering every story, every major character, and every pivotal event in the Doctor's televised chronology. You'll be tested with queries about cast, crew, guest stars, and production staff. You'll find questions about continuity, spin-offs, and even real-life historical figures and events which have played a significant role in the program's narrative. While no single volume could hold every detail of every episode of this enduring program, *The Wibbly-Wobbly, Timey-Wimey Trivia Quiz* will determine just how many details you, the fan, have stored in the pages of your mind.

First, however, let's establish the parameters of this exhaustive test. Please note that the questions herein pertain only to the televised *Doctor Who*, and do not extend to the "expanded universe" explored in novels, comics, audio dramas, and other media. If it is not shown, mentioned, or directly referenced in a TV episode, it is not, for the purposes of this book, considered canon. For this reason, you'll find no questions about popular literary companions like Bernice Summerfield or Frobisher the penguin, or non-televised adventures like the "Timewyrm" saga, "Scream of the Shalka," or the unfinished "Shada." While a few literary tales which have been adapted for TV are referenced, the questions herein refer specifically to the televised versions of those stories, not their printed source works.

In compiling the majority of questions and answers for this book, the only source required was the program itself. In cases where episodes or entire serials no longer exist, it was sometimes necessary to refer to reconstructions of the missing material, created with audio tracks recorded off-air and still images from the production. Though this tome is neither endorsed nor approved by the BBC, that agency's official *Doctor Who* website (www.bbc.co.uk/doctorwho) was consulted when broadcast dates or correct spellings of proper names required confirmation. For questions relating to additional cast and crew credits, the Internet Movie Database (www.imdb.com) was used as a primary source.

Dates and years mentioned herein are specifically stated or shown in the episodes in question, and no attempt has been made to fill in continuity gaps or explain apparent contradictions in chronology created by the disparate contributions of various writers, directors, actors, and script editors over the years. Ironing out such tricky matters is a bit beyond the scope of a simple trivia book like this one.

For the sake of consistency, a reasonably liberal definition of the word "companion" is employed in the questions and answers that follow. If a supporting character appears in more than one story, aids the Doctor in some way, and has traveled with him in the TARDIS, that character is herein considered a proper companion. Note that though the Doctor's ship was effectively inoperative through much of the single season Elizabeth "Liz" Shaw (Caroline John) spent as his U.N.I.T. assistant, the length of her tenure sufficiently qualifies her for the "companion" tag.

With all these things in mind, it's time to grab your Sonic Screwdriver, set the TARDIS coordinates, and dash off into *The Wibbly-Wobbly, Timey-Wimey Trivia Quiz*. Geronimo!

The First Doctor

1963-1966, 1973, 1983

THE ORIGINAL FIRST DOCTOR WAS VETERAN THESPIAN William Hartnell, best known before *Doctor Who* for leading roles in the films *Carry On Sergeant* (1958) and *This Sporting Life* (1963), and the TV comedy series *The Army Game*. Hartnell played the Doctor as an enigmatic, irascible, and highly inquisitive man of science. Initially disdainful of the humans who had forced their way into his TARDIS, the cantankerous, often mischievous First Doctor eventually came to trust and respect his Earth-born companions.

It was this mellower, more affectionate First Doctor that actor Richard Hurndall essayed in the twentieth-anniversary special, "The Five Doctors," produced eight years after Hartnell's untimely death. Reunited with his beloved granddaughter, Susan (again played by Carole Ann Ford), Hurndall's Time Lord was more compassionate than curmudgeonly, and displayed a tolerance for the eccentricities of his later selves not evident in his predecessor's final outing, the tenth-anniversary serial, "The Three Doctors."

The First Doctor succumbed to fatigue after battling the Cybermen, regenerating into a dramatically different version of himself.

"An Unearthly Child"

WRITERS: Anthony Coburn, C.E. Webber
DIRECTOR: Waris Hussein
STARS: William Hartnell, William Russell, Jacqueline Hill, Carole Ann Ford
ORIGINAL TRANSMISSION: 11/23-12/14/1963

An elderly man and his quirky teenage granddaughter transport two London schoolteachers to Earth's prehistory in a bizarre craft that looks like an ordinary London police box. Ford's stellar performance sets the tone in the opening moments, while the easy chemistry between Hill and Russell and the haughtiness of Hartnell's condescending Doctor dominate the rest of the proceedings. There's plenty of pulse-pounding prehistoric action in this fanciful fantasy adventure.

A. Prior to starring in *Doctor Who*, Carole Ann Ford appeared in the big-screen adaptation of what chilling John Wyndham science-fiction novel?

B. The first episode of *Doctor Who* was transmitted just one day after what tragic event?

C. According to school records, what is Susan Foreman's home address?

D. What fictional pop music group is referenced (and heard, courtesy of real-life band The Arthur Nelson Group) in this story's first episode?

E. What is the name of the cavewoman Hur's father?

"The Daleks"

WRITER: Terry Nation
DIRECTORS: Christopher Barry, Richard Martin
STARS: William Hartnell, William Russell, Jacqueline Hill, Carole Ann Ford
ORIGINAL TRANSMISSION: 12/21/1963-2/1/1964

Perhaps the most important science-fiction story in the history of television, this classic outing remains as engrossing today as it was nearly a half century ago. The TARDIS lands on the planet Skaro, where the

Doctor and his companions must convince the pacifistic Thals to fight for survival against the genocidal Daleks or be destroyed. Equally effective as a futuristic fable about fighting intolerance and an epic adventure in the tradition of 1940s movie serials, this timeless tale is still one of the most beloved and influential *Doctor Who* sagas of all time.

A. According to Susan, how many holes are there inside the lock of the TARDIS doors?

B. In which two later serials do the Thals appear?

C. What power source do the Daleks use to move around their city?

D. Guest star Virginia Wetherell went on to appear in what classic 1971 film, directed by Stanley Kubrick?

E. In which episode of "The Daleks" do the titular monsters first utter their signature catchphrase, "Exterminate!"?

"The Edge of Destruction"

WRITER: David Whitaker
DIRECTORS: Richard Martin, Frank Cox
STARS: William Hartnell, William Russell, Jacqueline Hill, Carole Ann Ford
ORIGINAL TRANSMISSION: 2/8-2/15/1964

When the TARDIS malfunctions, the Doctor and his companions suffer memory loss and begin to turn on one another. Claustrophobic atmosphere and intense performances make this budget-minded two-parter one of the darkest, most oppressive serials in the program's long history. Particularly memorable is the scene in which Hill's Barbara angrily chastises the Doctor after he accuses her and Ian of sabotage.

A. What planet does Susan say she and the Doctor visited "four or five journeys" before coming to 1963 Earth?

B. How many *Doctor Who* serials did David Whitaker write between 1963 and 1970?

C. Who attempts to strangle the Doctor from behind while he examines the malfunctioning TARDIS's control console?

D. What component of the Fast Return Switch causes the malfunction?

E. What do the Doctor and his companions find in the snow outside the TARDIS?

"Marco Polo"

WRITER: John Lucarotti
DIRECTORS: Waris Hussein, John Crockett
STARS: William Hartnell, William Russell, Jacqueline Hill, Carole Ann Ford
ORIGINAL TRANSMISSION: 2/22-4/4/1964

The earliest *Doctor Who* serial destroyed in the BBC's purge of the 1960s and '70s, this sprawling saga is one of the most sought-after of the missing tales. The Doctor and company help legendary explorer Marco Polo defeat a plot to assassinate Kublai Khan in thirteenth-century Mongolia. It's historical fantasy at its very best, highlighted by superb performances and a grand sense of adventure and intrigue. Guest star Mark Eden is excellent as the titular traveler.

A. What does Marco Polo hope to give to Kublai Khan (Martin Miller) in exchange for permission to return to Venice?

B. The Doctor beats Kublai Khan at what board game?

C. Guest star Zienia Merton appears forty-five years later in what unusual *Doctor Who* adventure?

D. What duplicitous member of Marco Polo's entourage intends to assassinate Kublai Khan?

E. Mark Eden is better known today for his role in what long-running British soap opera in the late 1980s?

"The Keys of Marinus"

WRITER: Terry Nation
DIRECTOR: John Gorrie
STARS: William Hartnell, William Russell, Jacqueline Hill, Carole Ann Ford
ORIGINAL TRANSMISSION: 4/11-5/16/1964

The TARDIS lands on the planet Marinus, where the Doctor and his companions must retrieve four hidden keys to a powerful machine before they fall into the hands of a ruthless villain (Stephen Dartnell). The first serial to incorporate multiple stories into a single, overarching narrative, this gritty adventure remains a superlative example of the oft-employed "quest" format. There is enough danger, intrigue, drama, and humor here to satisfy just about any fan.

A. What chemical designation appears on the bottle containing the second key?

B. Guest star Fiona Walker later appears as a villainous sorceress in what Seventh Doctor serial?

C. How many keys are needed to operate the Conscience of Marinus?

D. Of what instrument do the disembodied brains of Morphoton say, "No single mechanical device could reproduce its mobility and dexterity"?

E. What accomplished English actor, best known for a supporting role in Orson Welles' *Citizen Kane*, plays the ill-fated Arbitan?

"The Aztecs"

WRITER: John Lucarotti
DIRECTOR: John Crockett
STARS: William Hartnell, William Russell, Jacqueline Hill, Carole Ann Ford
ORIGINAL TRANSMISSION: 5/23-6/13/1964

In fifteenth-century Mexico, Barbara is mistaken for the female reincarnation of a legendary high priest and attempts to end the Aztec practice of human sacrifice. Another highlight for the versatile Hill, this thought-provoking epic is the first story to directly confront the dangers of altering history. Minus the threat of bug-eyed monsters, it's a very mature and personal tale that even includes the first on-screen romantic interest for the Doctor.

A. What is the name of the Aztec woman to whom the Doctor inadvertently gets engaged?

B. Barbara is mistaken for a female reincarnation of what ancient Aztec high priest?

C. What name is given to the young man selected to be sacrificed on the day of the next eclipse?

D. Actor John Ringham, who portrays the bloodthirsty Tlotoxl, also appears in "The Smugglers" and which Third Doctor serial?

E. Patrick Troughton's Second Doctor never met the Aztecs, but the actor himself played an evil high priest in what 1970s children's series about ancient Mexico?

"The Sensorites"

WRITER: Peter R. Newman
DIRECTORS: Mervyn Pinfield, Frank Cox
STARS: William Hartnell, William Russell, Jacqueline Hill, Carole Ann Ford
ORIGINAL TRANSMISSION: 6/20-8/1/1964

There's plenty of cosmic claustrophobia and intergalactic intrigue as our heroes navigate the confined corridors of an alien world, searching for the truth about a mysterious disease which is killing off the indigenous people. The titular, telepathic aliens are among the most sympathetic and memorable extraterrestrial beings in series' history. It's a tense and ambitious tale, marred only by a somewhat protracted running time and modest pacing.

A. According to Susan, plants on what planet communicate with one another using telepathy?

B. How many sashes does the Second Elder (Bartlett Mullins) wear across his chest?

C. What valuable mineral did humans originally come to the Sense-Sphere to collect?

D. Which regular cast member does not appear in Episodes Four and Five?

E. Co-director Frank Cox would go on to helm "Hear No Evil," a 1970 episode of what science-fiction series created by frequent *Doctor Who* writers Kit Pedler and Gerry Davis?

"The Reign of Terror"

WRITER: John Lucarotti
DIRECTORS: Henric Hirsch, John Gorrie
STARS: William Hartnell, William Russell, Jacqueline Hill, Carole Ann Ford
ORIGINAL TRANSMISSION: 8/8-9/12/1964

The Doctor and his companions visit France in 1794, where they meet a British spy and become embroiled in a plot to overthrow the ruthless dictator Robespierre (Keith Anderson). The first season of *Doctor Who* comes to a triumphant close in this enjoyable, exceptionally well-acted historical offering. Period authenticity, rich characterization, and a healthy dose of humor make this one a highlight of the Hartnell era.

A. Where do the Doctor and his companions initially believe they've landed?

B. The Doctor impersonates what government official in order to rescue his companions from prison?

C. Guest star Edward Brayshaw later appears as a villainous alien in what important Second Doctor serial?

D. In what earlier serial does Susan vocally criticize the accuracy of a book about the French Revolution?

E. With whom does Barras (John Law) conspire to bring down Robespierre?

"Planet of Giants"

WRITER: Louis Marks
DIRECTORS: Mervyn Pinfield, Douglas Camfield
STARS: William Hartnell, William Russell, Jacqueline Hill, Carole Ann Ford
ORIGINAL TRANSMISSION: 10/31-11/14/1964

Returning to contemporary Earth, the Doctor and his companions shrink to the size of insects and witness a brutal murder. This minor outing benefits from its excellent oversized props and truncated length, which contributes greatly to the increasing suspense as our heroes scramble to avoid the normal-sized antagonists and cure the poisoned Barbara. Though hardly a classic, it's engaging, effects-driven fun.

A. What is the name of the experimental new pesticide developed by Smithers and Forester?

B. Guest star Alan Tilvern later appears with Third Doctor actor Jon Pertwee's distant cousin, Bill Pertwee, in an episode of what comedy series?

C. What potentially catastrophic fault occurs in the TARDIS for only the second time?

D. What is the first "giant" creature the Doctor and his companions find after landing?

E. What prolific composer made his *Doctor Who* debut creating the incidental music for this story?

"The Dalek Invasion of Earth"

WRITER: Terry Nation
DIRECTOR: Richard Martin
STARS: William Hartnell, William Russell, Jacqueline Hill, Carole Ann Ford
ORIGINAL TRANSMISSION: 11/21-12/26/1964

"The Daleks" may have changed genre television forever, but it's this unequaled return engagement of the metal-shelled monsters from Skaro that set the standard by which all subsequent *Doctor Who* stories are measured to this day. The Doctor and his companions discover that twenty-second-century Earth has been conquered by the Daleks. Relentlessly grim and breathlessly paced, this action-packed masterpiece should be required viewing for anyone with an interest in horror, science-fiction, or TV history.

A. Guest star Nicholas Smith is best known today for playing Mr. Rumbold in what long-running British sitcom?

B. What horrific creature is the pet of the Black Dalek?

C. From what unusual location does the first Dalek shown on-screen make its entrance?

D. In order to stall her captors, Barbara tells the Black Dalek of an elaborate plot to overthrow them involving Red Indians, the Boston Tea Party, Robert E. Lee, and what Carthaginian military leader?

E. Susan Foreman would appear only once more in *Doctor Who*, in what Fifth Doctor adventure?

"The Rescue"

WRITER: David Whitaker
DIRECTOR: Christopher Barry
STARS: William Hartnell, William Russell, Jacqueline Hill, Maureen O'Brien
ORIGINAL TRANSMISSION: 1/2-1/9/1965

O'Brien makes a winning entrance in this brief but entertaining outing about survivors of an ill-fated starship crew terrorized by a malevolent alien monster on a remote planet. It's a compact, character-driven adventure that provides a perfect showcase for the leads, and proves for the first time that the program's format is flexible enough to endure major cast changes without missing a beat.

A. What fictitious actor is credited on-screen for playing the villainous Koquillion, in order to preserve the character's true identity in the story?

B. According to the Doctor, how many people lived on Dido when he last visited the planet?

C. What is Vicki's home planet?

D. What does Barbara use to slay the fierce-looking sand beast?

E. Vicki (Maureen O'Brien) says Barbara must be how old if she hails from 1963 Earth?

"The Romans"

WRITER: John Lucarotti
DIRECTOR: Christopher Barry
STARS: William Hartnell, William Russell, Jacqueline Hill, Maureen O'Brien
ORIGINAL TRANSMISSION: 1/16-2/6/1965

Broad comedy is the primary focus in this historical farce, in which the Doctor and his companions visit ancient Italy and meet Emperor Nero. Though the plot features assassinations, slave auctions, swordfights, and hard labor aboard a Roman galley, it's Hill's deft evasion of guest star Derek Francis' unwanted advances and the affectionate interplay between O'Brien and Hartnell that make this one so enjoyable.

A. What is the name of the famous musician for whom the Doctor is mistaken?

B. How much does Tavius (Michael Peake) pay for Barbara at the slave auction?

C. Derek Francis was a regular in what long-running comedy film series?

D. Delos is played by what frequent *Doctor Who* actor and stunt coordinator?

E. How do the Doctor and Vicki inadvertently influence history?

"The Web Planet"

WRITER: Bill Strutton
DIRECTOR: Richard Martin
STARS: William Hartnell, William Russell, Jacqueline Hill, Maureen O'Brien
ORIGINAL TRANSMISSION: 2/13-3/20/1965

On the planet Vortis, the Doctor and his companions help the moth-like Menoptra battle a malevolent alien force and its ant-like foot soldiers, the Zarbi. This off-beat, ambitious offering is a masterpiece of imagination and innovative production design, undone slightly by its overly somber tone and rather ponderous length. Hartnell has a grand time here, playing up the Doctor's natural curiosity and zest for discovery as he explores the story's bizarre locales.

A. Vrestin is played by what famed choreographer, who also created the unusual movements and speech patterns of the Menoptra?

B. What do the Doctor and his companions wear to protect themselves on the planet's surface?

C. What metal does the Animus use to channel its mind-controlling energy?

D. How were the Zarbi used by the Menoptra prior to the arrival of the Animus?

E. In what Ninth Doctor story is the Isop galaxy mentioned?

"The Crusade"

WRITER: David Whitaker
DIRECTOR: Douglas Camfield
STARS: William Hartnell, William Russell, Jacqueline Hill, Maureen O'Brien
ORIGINAL TRANSMISSION: 3/27-4/17/1965

In this riveting, star-studded saga, the Doctor and his companions land right in the middle of the conflict between the forces of King Richard the Lionheart (Julian Glover) and the Saracens. Cracking dialogue and first-rate performances keep this one moving along at a brisk pace at all times, rendering the numerous well-staged action sequences even more exhilarating. It's a gripping triumph of acting, atmosphere, and authenticity, ranking near the top of the list of the program's best historical efforts.

A. Jean Marsh, who plays Lady Joanna here, appears in which two later *Doctor Who* serials?

B. The TARDIS materializes in Palestine during which crusade?

C. What title is bestowed upon Ian by King Richard?

D. Julian Glover played the villain in what 1981 James Bond film?

E. What two future incarnations of the Doctor have been knighted by British royalty?

"The Space Museum"

WRITER: Glyn Jones
DIRECTOR: Mervyn Pinfield
STARS: William Hartnell, William Russell, Jacqueline Hill, Maureen O'Brien
ORIGINAL TRANSMISSION: 4/24-5/15/1965

In another showcase for the underrated Vicki, the Doctor and his companions land in a cosmic historical archive, only to discover that their future selves have become living exhibits. While the older members of the expedition grouse incessantly over how to handle their paradoxical predicament, O'Brien effectively steals the show by demonstrating her character's intellect and maturity in scene after scene. The plot itself is modestly diverting, but it's the bravura performance of the series' junior star that really distinguishes this outing.

A. For what purpose does Vicki truthfully tell the electronic brain that she needs weapons from the Morok armory?

B. The Doctor evades capture by hiding inside what museum exhibit?

C. Writer Glyn Jones appears in an on-camera role in what Fourth Doctor serial?

D. Guest star Jeremy Bulloch would later gain fame playing what villain in *The Empire Strikes Back* and *Return of the Jedi*?

E. Which aliens are shown monitoring the Doctor's TARDIS from a remote location as it departs the museum?

"The Chase"

WRITER: Terry Nation
DIRECTOR: Richard Martin
STARS: William Hartnell, William Russell, Jacqueline Hill, Maureen O'Brien, Peter Purves
ORIGINAL TRANSMISSION: 5/22-6/26/1965

The Doctor and his companions are pursued across time and space by the Daleks, who have constructed their own extradimensional craft. Often criticized for injecting humor into the growing Dalek mythos, this sweeping six-parter is actually great fun throughout. From the shocking revelation about the fate of the *Marie Celeste* to the final battle with the globular Mechanoids, this is an action-packed, wholly engaging final foray for Hill and Russell.

A. Prior to making his debut as Steven in the final episode of this story, actor Peter Purves had a brief cameo as an American tourist in what *Doctor Who* serial?

B. What do the Daleks create in their Cell Renovator Chamber?

C. What real-life British rock group appears briefly on the Time-Space Visualizer?

D. In what region of the planet Aridius does the TARDIS land?

E. Shortly after appearing as Frankenstein's monster in this serial, guest star John Maxim had an uncredited role as a police sergeant in what Hammer Frankenstein film?

"The Time Meddler"

WRITER: Dennis Spooner
DIRECTOR: Douglas Camfield
STARS: William Hartnell, Maureen O'Brien, Peter Purves
ORIGINAL TRANSMISSION: 7/3-7/24/1965

Guest star Peter Butterworth delivers an unforgettable performance as the Monk, a member of the Doctor's own species determined to alter the course of Earth history by intervening in the Norman conquest of England. Given a worthy foil, Hartnell chews the scenery with aplomb. This otherwise light-hearted effort features one of the series' darkest moments, involving an implied assault by Viking raiders on a defenseless Saxon woman (Alethea Charlton).

A. What monument does the Monk claim to have helped the ancient Britons build by giving them an anti-gravitational lift?

B. The Monk hopes to alter the outcome of what historic conflict?

C. Alethea Charlton previously appeared in what early *Doctor Who* serial?

D. Gunnar the Giant is played by what 6'8" actor, best known for playing the towering bodyguard of villain Ernst Stavro Blofeld in *You Only Live Twice*?

E. What minor change to the acronym TARDIS, resulting from Vicki's explanation of the abbreviation, is introduced in "The Time Meddler" and would remain through most of the original series?

"Galaxy 4"

WRITER: William Emms
DIRECTOR: Derek Martinus
STARS: William Hartnell, Maureen O'Brien, Peter Purves
ORIGINAL TRANSMISSION: 9/11-10/2/1965

The Doctor and his companions fight intolerance as they attempt to rescue two groups of shipwrecked space travelers from a doomed planet. Solid production values and a strong moral message are highlights of this lost tale, which challenges perceptions with its beautiful, blonde antagonists and ugly, reptilian good guys. Overlooked and often forgotten, it's actually a solid start to Hartnell's third year in the TARDIS.

A. What nickname does Vicki give to the Rills' robotic servants?

B. Who plays Maaga, the beautiful but ruthless leader of the Drahvins?

C. Though William Emms wrote scripts for several television series in the 1960s and '70s, what was his primary occupation?

D. What toxic chemical do the Rills breathe?

E. Though not shown, the Drahvins are said to be among many alien races whose fleets are approaching Earth in what Eleventh Doctor story?

"Mission to the Unknown"

WRITER: Terry Nation
DIRECTOR: Derek Martinus
STARS: Edward de Souza, Barry Jackson, Jeremy Young, Robert Cartland
ORIGINAL TRANSMISSION: 10/9/1965

A team of intrepid Space Security Service agents battle Daleks and poisonous walking plants on the planet Kembel. Though it's the only *Doctor Who* tale not to feature any of the series' regular cast members, this lively bit of Saturday matinee fantasy is quite enjoyable in its own right. Imaginative production design and overpowering atmosphere effectively set the stage for the upcoming serial, "The Daleks' Master Plan," for which this single-episode entry is a prequel.

A. What is the name of the murderous, ambulatory vegetation the Daleks bring to Kembel from their home world?

B. What actor who does not appear in "Mission to the Unknown" is still listed in the closing credits?

C. This was the final episode for what founding *Doctor Who* producer?

D. What happens to Garvey (Barry Jackson) and Lowery (Jeremy Young) after coming in contact with the deadly plants?

E. "Mission to the Unknown" is one of only three *Doctor Who* serials of which no footage survives. What are the other two?

"The Myth Makers"

WRITER: Donald Cotton
DIRECTOR: Michael Leeston-Smith
STARS: William Hartnell, Maureen O'Brien, Peter Purves, Adrienne Hill
ORIGINAL TRANSMISSION: 10/16-11/6/1965

In this lighter entry, the Doctor and his companions are forced to assist the ancient Greeks in their efforts to capture the city of Troy. Sharp dialogue and stand-out performances abound, with O'Brien doing some of her finest work in her final outing. As in "The Romans" in the previous season, historical accuracy takes a back seat to humor, resulting in an energetic period piece which is more entertaining than educational.

A. Vicki adopts what name after falling for Troilus (James Lynn)?

B. What actor portrays famed hero Odysseus?

C. The Greeks initially believe the Doctor is what god in disguise?

D. Just prior to joining *Doctor Who*, new producer John Wiles served as the script editor for what cloak-and-dagger TV mini-series?

E. How long has Troy been under siege when the Doctor and his companions arrive on the plains of Asia Minor?

"The Daleks' Master Plan"

WRITERS: Terry Nation, Dennis Spooner
DIRECTOR: Douglas Camfield
STARS: William Hartnell, Peter Purves, Adrienne Hill, Jean Marsh
ORIGINAL TRANSMISSION: 11/13/1965-1/29/1966

The fourth Dalek tale of the Hartnell era is a satisfying return to the more serious tone of the first two. The Doctor and his allies must disrupt an evil galactic alliance, expose a traitor, and prevent the Daleks from using a doomsday weapon known as a Time Destructor. Its epic length works against it at times, but this monumental mega-serial features too many familiar faces, fine performances, and memorable milestones to be anything other than an unqualified masterpiece of small-screen space opera.

A. Katarina (Adrienne Hill) is the first of only two companions in series' history to join the TARDIS crew in one story only to depart forever in the next. Who is the other?

B. What actor, best known for playing Brigadier Lethbridge-Stewart in numerous *Doctor Who* stories, appears here as Space Security Service officer Brett Vyon?

C. What other member of the Doctor's own species appears in this serial?

D. Kevin Stoney, who plays the Daleks' duplicitous ally Mavic Chen, aids the Cybermen in which epic Second Doctor serial?

E. Mavic Chen's spacecraft is called a what?

"The Massacre of St. Bartholomew's Eve"

WRITERS: John Lucarotti, Donald Tosh
DIRECTOR: Paddy Russell
STARS: William Hartnell, Peter Purves, Jackie Lane
ORIGINAL TRANSMISSION: 2/5-2/26/1966

The Doctor and Steven become embroiled in the affairs of the Huguenots on the eve of the brutal slaughter of thousands of Protestants in sixteenth-century France. Hartnell (in a dual role as the Time Lord and a cold-blooded Catholic dignitary) and Purves are both magnificent in a somber and serious-minded effort that pulls few punches when confronted with its rather mature subject matter.

A. What is Dodo's real first name?

B. The Doctor is a perfect double for what church leader?

C. "The Massacre of St. Bartholomew's Eve" is not the first serial to begin with the Doctor having only one travelling companion, but it is the first in which the lone companion is what?

D. How long after the end of Third French War of Religion did the St. Bartholomew's Day Massacre take place?

E. In what year does Dodo (Jackie Lane) enter the TARDIS?

"The Ark"

WRITERS: Paul Erickson, Lesley Scott
DIRECTOR: Michael Imison
STARS: William Hartnell, Peter Purves, Jackie Lane
ORIGINAL TRANSMISSION: 3/5-3/26/1966

The Doctor and his companions inadvertently spark an uprising aboard a spaceship carrying the last humans and their alien servants to a new home planet. This well-designed offering is remembered today primarily for the mop-topped, cyclopean Monoids, perhaps the most unusual looking monsters in the program's long history. Underappreciated by fans and critics, it's a clever, action-oriented tale that delivers plenty of pulp-style thrills.

A. What co-creator of the Cybermen began his tenure as the program's full-time script editor with this serial?

B. What veteran film and TV actor provides the voice of the invisible Refusian?

C. How much time passes between the Doctor's first and second visits to the Ark?

D. Where does the skeptical Dodo initially believe the TARDIS has landed?

E. Contradicting the events of this story, Earth is later shown being destroyed by the expanding sun in the year 5 Billion in what Ninth Doctor story?

"The Celestial Toymaker"

WRITERS: Brian Hayles, Donald Tosh
DIRECTOR: Bill Sellars
STARS: William Hartnell, Peter Purves, Jackie Lane
ORIGINAL TRANSMISSION: 4/2-4/23/1966

In this fantastic departure from typical science-fiction and historical plots, the Doctor and his companions arrive in a strange realm where a god-like being forces them to play lethal versions of children's games. Guest star Michael Gough is excellent as the mysterious, malevolent Toymaker. This unusual outing's only major weakness is the protracted presentation of some of the game sequences involving Steven and Dodo.

A. What is the final game Steven and Dodo are forced by the Toymaker to play?

B. In exactly how many moves must the Trilogic Game be completed?

C. Who supervises the game in which Steven and Dodo must find a key in Mrs. Wiggs' kitchen?

D. Michael Gough later appears as a treacherous Time Lord in what Fifth Doctor story?

E. Writer Brian Hayles went on to create what recurring alien race in *Doctor Who*?

"The Gunfighters"

WRITER: Donald Cotton
DIRECTOR: Rex Tucker
STARS: William Hartnell, Peter Purves, Jackie Lane
ORIGINAL TRANSMISSION: 4/30-5/21/1966

The most infamous *Doctor Who* story of all is indeed the weakest of the Hartnell era, but is considerably more enjoyable than most fans are willing to admit. The Doctor and company meet Doc Holliday (Anthony Jacobs) and Wyatt Earp (John Alderson) on the eve of their legendary showdown with the Clanton brothers. Historical inaccuracies and dodgy American accents do little to dampen the fun. The real problem is the omnipresent musical narration, a tiresome device that frequently distracts from the high-spirited action.

A. What performer sings the ongoing ballad which serves as narration for this story?

B. "The Gunfighters" was the last classic *Doctor Who* serial to feature what designations?

C. What unusual ornament hangs outside Doc Holliday's practice in Tombstone?

D. What pseudonym does the Doctor use when introducing himself to Wyatt Earp?

E. What is the reward offered for Johnny Ringo (Laurence Payne) in Dodge City?

"The Savages"

WRITER: Ian Stuart Black
DIRECTOR: Christopher Barry
STARS: William Hartnell, Peter Purves, Jackie Lane
ORIGINAL TRANSMISSION: 5/28-6/18/1966

In the distant future, the Doctor and his companions visit an idyllic society which is sustained by draining the individual life forces of the savages who inhabit a nearby wilderness. Though not highly regarded by fans and critics, this futuristic morality play boasts a thought-provoking premise and a superb performance from the departing Purves.

Also noteworthy is the fine turn of villain Frederick Jaeger, who expertly mimics Hartnell's voice and mannerisms after his character absorbs part of the Doctor's personality.

A. The Elders know of the Doctor upon his arrival, and refer to him as what?

B. Who are the leaders of the Savages?

C. Guest stars Frederick Jaeger and Ewen Solon also appear together in what Fourth Doctor story?

D. What gift do the Elders give to Dodo?

E. Christopher Barry later directed what unofficial, direct-to-video spin-off of *Doctor Who,* starring Nicholas Courtney, Elisabeth Sladen, and Deborah Watling?

"The War Machines"

WRITER: Ian Stuart Black
DIRECTOR: Michael Ferguson
STARS: William Hartnell, Jackie Lane, Michael Craze, Anneke Wills
ORIGINAL TRANSMISSION: 6/25-7/16/1966

Lane makes a relatively inauspicious exit midway through this excellent, Quatermass-style tale of a defense supercomputer gaining sentience in contemporary London, simply disappearing from the story and allowing Wills' Polly and Craze's Ben to take center stage. The new companions acquit themselves nicely, however, and the scenes of soldiers battling homicidal robots in modern alleys and warehouses foreshadow the Earth-based monster mashes of the Second and Third Doctor eras.

A. What does the acronym WOTAN stand for?

B. What British landmark is the primary setting for this story?

C. The sentient WOTAN is the only character in series history to directly refer to the Doctor by what name?

D. How many war machines have WOTAN's enslaved workers built?

E. What real-life BBC TV news anchor plays himself in this serial?

"The Smugglers"

WRITER: Brian Hayles
DIRECTOR: Julia Smith
STARS: William Hartnell, Michael Craze, Anneke Wills
ORIGINAL TRANSMISSION: 9/10-10/1/1966

In seventeenth-century Cornwall, the Doctor and his companions run afoul of pirates in search of lost treasure. Extensive location shooting and excellent sets give the penultimate tale of the First Doctor era an air of big-screen spectacle, but it's crisp writing and strong performances that elevate this swashbuckling saga above its inherent clichés. Michael Godfrey and George A. Cooper are delightfully diabolical as the colorful villains of this engaging adventure.

A. "The Smugglers" holds what dubious distinction among First Doctor serials?

B. What is the angelic-sounding name of Pike's murderous henchman?

C. The Doctor aids Joseph Longfoot (Terence De Marney) with what painful ailment?

D. Pike's missing left hand has been replaced by what menacing object?

E. Prior to appearing in this serial, Terence De Marney guest-starred in what 1962 episode of Rod Serling's *The Twilight Zone*?

"The Tenth Planet"

WRITERS: Kit Pedler, Gerry Davis
DIRECTOR: Derek Martinus
STARS: William Hartnell, Michael Craze, Anneke Wills, Patrick Troughton
ORIGINAL TRANSMISSION: 10/8-10/29/1966

This suspenseful, sensational debut of the sinister Cybermen would be a perfect close to the Hartnell era if the actor hadn't been too ill to play much of a part in the proceedings. As it is, the story is a fine showcase for the sublimely creepy metal monsters, the superb acting of Wills and Craze, and the wholesale scenery-chomping of guest star Robert Beatty, as a bellicose American general. Even in the wake of so many similar scenes to follow, the sight of the Doctor morphing into an entirely new man is nothing short of surreal.

A. Guest star John Brandon would later appear in an episode of what short-lived American science-fiction series about a quirky explorer and his youthful sidekick traveling through time, fixing errors in history?

B. What powerful device do the Cybermen plan to employ to destroy the Earth?

C. General Cutler's son (Callen Angelo) is sent on a mission to rescue what doomed spacecraft?

D. Ben discovers that the Cybermen are vulnerable to what?

E. In how many episodes of "The Tenth Planet" does William Hartnell appear?

(Answers begin on Page 213.)

The Second Doctor

1966-1969, 1973, 1983, 1985

PRIOR TO BEING CAST AS THE DOCTOR, PATRICK TROUGHTON was an accomplished character actor with dozens of stage and television credits to his name. After leaving the series at the end of the sixth season, the versatile performer continued to work steadily in television right up until his death in 1987. He also appeared in many Hammer horror films in the early 1970s, usually playing grave robbers and other undesirable types. Troughton returned to the role of the Doctor three times, in "The Three Doctors," "The Five Doctors," and finally "The Two Doctors."

The Second Doctor is most often characterized as a bumbling, somewhat absent-minded cosmic hobo. In truth, Troughton's Time Lord was perhaps the sharpest and most calculating of them all. Though prone to slapstick and comedic interplay with his companions, Troughton's broad performance was underscored with moments of great cunning and ingenuity, and he could deliver somber news with a gravitas unequaled by his successors.

After thwarting yet another alien invasion, the Second Doctor was recalled to his home planet, where he stood trial for interfering in the affairs of other planets. As punishment for his crimes, he was banished to Earth and forced to regenerate.

"Power of the Daleks"

WRITER: David Whitaker
DIRECTOR: Christopher Barry
STARS: Patrick Troughton, Michael Craze, Anneke Wills
ORIGINAL TRANSMISSION: 11/5-12/10/1966

On the planet Vulcan, the Doctor and his companions try to convince a curious scientist that the alien "robots" he's reactivated are actually murderous Daleks. One of the finest Dalek tales of all, this expertly acted potboiler cleverly exploits the viewer's knowledge to ramp up the tension as guest star Robert James stumbles toward disaster, and Ben and Polly try to determine if they can trust the quirky man claiming to be the regenerated Doctor.

A. Where on the planet Vulcan do the Doctor and his companions land?

B. Guest star Robert Luckham is the son of what veteran actor, who later appears as the White Guardian in a Fifth Doctor serial?

C. How many Daleks does Lesterson initially find in the downed space capsule?

D. What actor, best known for his later voiceover work in *Danger Mouse* and *Wallace and Gromit: The Curse of the Were-Rabbit*, plays Resno, the unfortunate lab assistant "accidentally" gunned down by a reactivated Dalek?

E. Who kills Governor Hensell (Peter Bathurst)?

"The Highlanders"

WRITERS: Elwyn Jones, Gerry Davis
DIRECTOR: Hugh David
STARS: Patrick Troughton, Michael Craze, Anneke Wills, Frazer Hines
ORIGINAL TRANSMISSION: 12/17/1966-1/7/1967

Devoid of science-fiction and fantasy elements, this pure historical adventure relies on action and fine performances. The Doctor and his friends run afoul of the British Army in eighteenth-century Scotland. Hines ably demonstrates the tenacity, fearlessness, amiability, and deft comic timing that would eventually make Jamie a fan favorite companion in his rugged, rousing debut. Guest player Michael Elwyn is fun as the foppish Redcoat, Lt. Algernon Ffinch.

A. What is Jamie's father's name?

B. Guest star Donald Bisset would go on to appear in the 1978 fantasy adventure film *Warlords of the Deep*, which was written by what frequent *Doctor Who* scribe?

C. The Doctor introduces himself by what pseudonym in the first episode of this serial?

D. What is the name of Captain Trask's ship?

E. Michael Elwyn appears in a recurring role in what 2006-2009 adventure series, which also stars Patrick Troughton's grandson, Sam?

"The Underwater Menace"

WRITER: Geoffrey Orme
DIRECTOR: Julia Smith
STARS: Patrick Troughton, Michael Craze, Anneke Wills, Frazer Hines
ORIGINAL TRANSMISSION: 1/14-2/4/1967

The Doctor and his companions visit the lost continent of Atlantis, where a mad scientist is creating mutant fish-people from the survivors of shipwrecks. Oft-criticized for its *Flash Gordon* sensibilities and rather silly monsters, this is actually a fun little pulp adventure, rich with cartoon villainy and plenty of camp humor. It may be the weakest serial of the Troughton era, but it's broad and outlandish enough to satisfy fans of classic B-movie cheese.

A. In what ninth-season story does the Third Doctor visit Atlantis?

B. Which episode of this serial is the earliest surviving *Doctor Who* episode starring Patrick Troughton?

C. What Atlantean priest aids the Doctor in warning the King of Professor Zaroff's evil intentions?

D. How does Zaroff (Joseph Furst) plan to raise Atlantis back to the surface?

E. Guest star Peter Stephens previously appeared in what unusual First Doctor serial, portraying a character reminiscent of Charles Hamilton's rotund comic hero, Billy Bunter?

"The Moonbase"

WRITER: Kit Pedler
DIRECTOR: Morris Barry
STARS: Patrick Troughton, Michael Craze, Anneke Wills, Frazer Hines
ORIGINAL TRANSMISSION: 2/11-3/4/1967

The Cybermen were the preeminent villains of the Second Doctor's tenure, and this triumphant return of the metal men from Mondas is a big part of the reason why. The Time Lord and his companions visit a weather control station on the moon, only to discover it has been infiltrated by Cybermen bent on using it to conquer Earth. Hines' role is reduced here, but he makes the most of his few scenes. Wills proves her mettle as a top scream queen of the 1960s as she is menaced repeatedly by mechanical monstrosities.

A. What is the name of the device used by the Moonbase crew to control Earth's weather?

B. Guest star Alan Rowe appears in what two Fourth Doctor serials?

C. Which Moonbase crewmember is the first to contract the "virus" that's spreading throughout the station?

D. Guest star André Maranne appears with future *Doctor Who* lead Peter Davison in what episode of the long-running series *All Creatures Great and Small*?

E. The Cybermen gain access to the Moonbase through a hole in the wall of what compartment?

"The Macra Terror"

WRITER: Ian Stuart Black
DIRECTOR: John Davies
STARS: Patrick Troughton, Michael Craze, Anneke Wills, Frazer Hines
ORIGINAL TRANSMISSION: 3/11-4/1/1967

In this smart, scary outing, the Doctor and his companions visit a seemingly idyllic holiday camp that is actually run by malevolent, mind-controlling giant crabs. "The Happiness Patrol" and "The Long Game" would explore similar themes decades later, but this early outing easily trumps both with its mammoth monsters and first-rate performances. Sadly available only in audio, print, and reconstructed forms, this remains one of the sharpest and most engaging allegorical offerings in series' history.

A. What element was first added to the opening title sequence for this serial, and would remain part of the classic series' opening through its final episode in 1989?

B. What piercing sound breaks the Macra's mental hold over Ben?

C. What two actresses played the role of Chicki, which was recast after the first episode for contractual reasons?

D. The Doctor and his companions are sentenced to join what group working in the most hazardous part of the mine?

E. Guest star Peter Jeffrey appears as the intrepid Inspector Trout in what pair of darkly comedic Vincent Price chillers?

"The Faceless Ones"

WRITERS: David Ellis, Malcolm Hulke
DIRECTOR: Gerry Mill
STARS: Patrick Troughton, Michael Craze, Anneke Wills, Frazer Hines
ORIGINAL TRANSMISSION: 4/8-5/13/1967

Face-changing aliens poses as travel agents to lure in unsuspecting humans and steal their identities in this enjoyable final journey for Wills and Craze. Though the plot is rather absurd, the Chameleons themselves are quite creepy, and the dialogue is especially sharp throughout. The result is a suspenseful and well-acted outing that foreshadows the style and tone of the program through much of the decade to come.

A. Guest star Wanda Ventham later appears in what Seventh Doctor story, set on the planet Lakertya?

B. What is the name of the tour agency operated by the aliens?

C. In what real-life London airport does this serial take place?

D. What actress, who plays Liverpudlian teenager Samantha Briggs, declined an invitation by producers to join the series after this story as a full-time companion?

E. What happens to the TARDIS at the end of the serial?

"The Evil of the Daleks"

WRITER: David Whitaker
DIRECTORS: Derek Martinus, Timothy Combe
STARS: Patrick Troughton, Frazer Hines, Deborah Watling
ORIGINAL TRANSMISSION: 5/20-7/1/1967

In the most unusual and intelligent Dalek tale of the 1960s, the monsters from Skaro hold a young girl captive and force Jamie to undergo a grueling experiment to rescue her, in order to isolate the factors that differentiate Daleks from humans. Watling makes an impressive debut as Victoria, the original series' premiere damsel in distress, while the scene featuring the Doctor playing with child-like, humanized Daleks is both funny and touching. The influence of this, the first appearance of the towering Dalek Emperor, is still being felt in Dalek stories today.

A. How many mirrors are employed in Theodore Maxtible's time cabinet?

B. Guest star Sonny Caldinez is best known for playing members of what towering alien race in four later *Doctor Who* serials?

C. Maxtible (Marius Goring) hopes to gain the secrets of what chemical process?

D. What are the names given to the three humanized Daleks?

E. Mirrors are later used to construct a time machine in what Tenth Doctor story?

"The Tomb of the Cybermen"

WRITERS: Kit Pedler, Gerry Davis
DIRECTOR: Morris Barry
STARS: Patrick Troughton, Frazer Hines, Deborah Watling
ORIGINAL TRANSMISSION: 9/2-9/23/1967

On the planet Telos, the Doctor and his companions join an archaeological expedition into a massive cavern where the Cybermen hibernate. This thoroughly spectacular outing is best remembered for chilling monsters and breathtaking visuals, but its greatest strength is the tour de force performance of Troughton. He deftly trades comic banter with Hines, warmly comforts the frightened Watling, and cleverly manipulates multiple villains with equal ease, shifting effortlessly from clown to ringmaster as he steals the show again and again.

A. The Doctor tells Jamie and Victoria he is how old?

B. Guest star Roy Stewart later appears in what 1971 Hammer vampire film with Peter Cushing, star of both big-screen *Doctor Who* movies in the 1960s?

C. This serial features the debut of what mechanical servants of the Cybermen?

D. Klieg (George Pastell) and Kaftan (Shirley Cooklin) belong to what intellectual organization?

E. Shirley Cooklin was married to what member of the *Doctor Who* production team at the time this serial was produced?

"The Abominable Snowmen"

WRITERS: Mervyn Haisman, Henry Lincoln
DIRECTOR: Gerald Blake
STARS: Patrick Troughton, Frazer Hines, Deborah Watling
ORIGINAL TRANSMISSION: 9/30-11/4/1967

In this exceptionally well-written and atmospheric tale, the Doctor and his companions battle robotic Yetis and an incorporeal alien entity in Tibet in the 1930s. There is perhaps no more revered or coveted lost serial from the Troughton era, and listening to the audio track or reading the Target novelization will quickly reveal why. The performances are sharp throughout, the mountainside locations and monastery sets equally excellent, and the titular titans unforgettable.

A. What holy relic does the Doctor intend to return to the Detsen Monastery?

B. The actor who portrays Professor Travers in this serial and "The Web of Fear" is the real-life father of which regular cast member?

C. Guest star Wolfe Morris appeared a decade earlier in what similarly titled Hammer horror film about the Yeti?

D. What children's song does the Doctor play on his recorder in this serial?

E. What does Professor Travers see just as the Doctor and his companions prepare to depart in the TARDIS?

"The Ice Warriors"

WRITER: Brian Hayles
DIRECTOR: Derek Martinus
STARS: Patrick Troughton, Frazer Hines, Deborah Watling
ORIGINAL TRANSMISSION: 11/11-12/16/1967

In a future ice age, scientists at a base designed to slow the advance of glaciers on Britain uncover the frozen body of a huge, reptilian Martian. The Ice Warriors are stunning, towering creatures that wholly deserve to be ranked among the greatest *Doctor Who* monsters of all time. This tense tale provides an excellent showcase for the screaming skills of Watling, and makes a compelling statement about man's overreliance on technology in our increasingly turbulent world.

A. What device is used by the crew of Brittanicus Base to control the ice floes?

B. Though not shown or directly involved in the action, the Ice Warriors are mentioned in what Tenth Doctor story?

C. Guest star Wendy Gifford also appears in what 1967 episode of the science-fiction spy series *Adam Adamant Lives!*, directed by Ridley Scott?

D. What weapon do the Ice Warriors intend to use in their attack on the Brittanicus Base?

E. Frequent guest star Roy Skelton, best known for voicing Daleks and Cybermen throughout the original series, provides the voice for what in this serial?

"The Enemy of the World"

WRITER: David Whitaker
DIRECTOR: Barry Letts
STARS: Patrick Troughton, Frazer Hines, Deborah Watling
ORIGINAL TRANSMISSION: 12/23/1967-1/27/1968

The evil twin is a standard plot device for long-running genre TV shows, but few series have had the luxury of having such a versatile and gifted lead actor to tackle the dual role of benevolent hero and malevolent doppelganger as this one. Troughton is in top form twice over in this 007-inspired action epic which sees the Doctor and his companions facing off against a ruthless dictator with a very familiar face in Earth's not-too-distant future. There's even a leggy blonde "Bond girl," in the form of Mary Peach's sexy super agent Astrid Perrier.

A. How is the Doctor able to mimic the voice and mannerisms of Salamander?

B. What longtime BBC Head of Drama, who played a vital role in the creation of *Doctor Who*, left his position shortly after the completion of this serial?

C. Guest star Milton Johns later appears as an opportunistic Gallifreyan Castellan in what Fourth Doctor serial?

D. Victoria is appointed to what post in Salamander's administration?

E. Barry Letts co-created what short-lived 1970s science-fiction series about a twenty-first-century lunar colony with another frequent *Doctor Who* contributor, Terrence Dicks?

"The Web of Fear"

WRITERS: Mervyn Haisman, Henry Lincoln
DIRECTOR: Douglas Camfield
STARS: Patrick Troughton, Frazer Hines, Deborah Watling, Nicholas Courtney
ORIGINAL TRANSMISSION: 2/3-3/9/1968

The Yeti returns in a modern-day sequel that somehow manages to top its classic predecessor for spine-tingling thrills and chills. The Doctor and his companions find contemporary London in a state of emergency, as mysterious webs fill the underground railway tunnels and hairy, homicidal monsters wander the streets. Claustrophobic locations and a well-crafted mystery plot thread keep this one hopping along at a nice clip. Courtney's Lethbridge-Stewart debuts, making this the prototype for the U.N.I.T. tales to come.

A. What rank does Lethbridge-Stewart hold in this serial?

B. Who plays Professor Travers' daughter, Anne?

C. Guest star John Levene, who plays a Cyberman in "The Moonbase" and a robotic Yeti here, portrays what popular recurring character in the U.N.I.T. stories of the late 1960s and early '70s?

D. What device does the Great Intelligence hope to use in order to drain the Doctor's mind?

E. What object is found in Captain Knight's pocket after he is killed?

"Fury from the Deep"

WRITER: Victor Pemberton
DIRECTOR: Hugh David
STARS: Patrick Troughton, Frazer Hines, Deborah Watling
ORIGINAL TRANSMISSION: 3/16-4/20/1968

Fans and historians discussing this lost serial tend to focus on the clever use of first-rate screamer Watling's vocal talents to defeat the monsters in the closing moments. What is sadly forgotten is the fact that writer Pemberton and director Hughes are able to craft an extremely suspenseful and shiver-inducing tale in which the inhuman menace is little more than soap bubbles and seaweed. It's an exceptionally inventive and atmospheric send off for Victoria, worthy of a place among the scariest *Doctor Who* stories of all time.

A. Where does the TARDIS land at the beginning of the story?

B. What sound does the Doctor believe he hears coming from within the gas pipe?

C. Guest star Margaret John, who plays Euro Sea Gas Director Megan Jones here, later appears in what 2006 Tenth Doctor story?

D. What iconic device makes its debut in the first episode of this serial?

E. Writer Victor Pemberton earlier appeared on-camera (in a non-speaking role) in what Second Doctor serial?

"The Wheel in Space"

WRITER: David Whitaker
DIRECTOR: Tristan de Vere Cole
STARS: Patrick Troughton, Frazer Hines, Wendy Padbury
ORIGINAL TRANSMISSION: 4/27-6/1/1968

The Cybermen infiltrate a space station, hoping to use it as a radio beacon to guide a planned invasion of Earth. In truth, this is little more than a protracted remake of "The Moonbase," with more impressive sets and more corridors for the Mondasian monstrosities to lumber down. What sets it apart is the introduction of the Doctor's bright, bubbly new companion, Zoe Herriot, played brilliantly by the effervescent Padbury.

A. What is the official call sign of Space Station W3, aka the Wheel?

B. Wendy Padbury went on to become a theatrical agent, representing former *Doctor Who* actors Nicholas Courtney, Colin Baker, and what 1980s companion actor?

C. What is Zoe's official job title aboard the Wheel?

D. What does Jamie use to sabotage the x-ray laser?

E. This serial features the first use by the Doctor of what common-sounding alias?

"The Dominators"

WRITER: Norman Ashby
DIRECTOR: Morris Barry
STARS: Patrick Troughton, Frazer Hines, Wendy Padbury
ORIGINAL TRANSMISSION: 8/10-9/7/1968

A pair of evil aliens and their murderous robot servants plot to superheat the core of the peaceful planet Dulkis, turning it into a massive fuel source for their fleet. This one is a bit overlong and budget-constrained for its own good, but the Dominators' lethal automatons are nice additions to a long line of mechanical monsters in *Doctor Who*, and guest stars Ronald Allen and Kenneth Ives deliver fine turns as the sadistic, contentious would-be conquerors.

A. What are the Dominators' deadly robots called?

B. Guest star Brian Cant previously appeared as an injured intergalactic policeman in what First Doctor serial?

C. How long has it been since the last nuclear explosion occurred on the Island of Death?

D. "Norman Ashby" is a pseudonym for frequent *Doctor Who* writer Mervyn Haisman and what author, best known for co-writing the controversial book *The Holy Blood and the Holy Grail*?

E. Arthur Cox, who plays Cully here, later appears as a befuddled old man who momentarily runs afoul of Amy Pond in what Eleventh Doctor story?

"The Mind Robber"

WRITERS: Derrick Sherwin, Peter Ling
DIRECTOR: David Maloney
STARS: Patrick Troughton, Frazer Hines, Wendy Padbury
ORIGINAL TRANSMISSION: 9/14-10/12/1968

In the most unusual story of the Second Doctor years, the Time Lord and his companions are pulled into an alternate dimension where fictional characters are real, and a mysterious writer creates deadly creatures with his typewriter. Alternately surreal and silly, this engaging offering provides a fine showcase for the actors, and proves that the series' flexible format can be stretched well beyond the limits of ordinary science-fiction television without missing a beat.

A. Jamie is the first of four *Doctor Who* companions to be played by more than one actor. Who are the other three?

B. What non-existent weapon is yielded by the superhero Karkus (Christopher Robbie)?

C. The Doctor later encounters variations of the monstrous Minotaur in which two serials?

D. The white robots that menace the Doctor and his companions originally appeared in an episode of what British science-fiction anthology series?

E. Bernard Horsfall, who portrays Jonathan Swift's Lemuel Gulliver in this serial, later appears as a treacherous Time Lord in what Fourth Doctor serial?

"The Invasion"

WRITER: Derrick Sherwin
DIRECTOR: Douglas Camfield
STARS: Patrick Troughton, Frazer Hines, Wendy Padbury, Nicholas Courtney
ORIGINAL TRANSMISSION: 11/2-12/21/1968

In the grandest, most gripping Cybermen story of all, an ambitious electronics manufacturer conspires with the malevolent metallic aliens to conquer the Earth. Epic in scope and action-packed from beginning to end, this all-time classic literally does for the Cybermen what "The Dalek Invasion of Earth" did for the villainous pepper pots from Skaro. Kevin Stoney and Peter Halliday are superlative villains, U.N.I.T. makes a triumphant formal debut, and the scenes of Cybermen marching through modern-day London are simply terrifying.

A. What electronics firm is run by the villainous Tobias Vaughn (Kevin Stoney)?

B. Leggy guest star Sally Faulkner went on to appear in the 1974 lesbian vampire thriller *Vampyres*, and a two-part episode of what short-lived 1990s horror series about a female lycanthrope?

C. Where does the Cyber Director indicate that the Cybermen may have previously encountered the Doctor?

D. Frequent guest star Peter Halliday's last *Doctor Who* appearance to date occurs in the second episode of what Seventh Doctor serial?

E. In which episode of "The Invasion" does Wendy Padbury not appear?

"The Krotons"

WRITER: Robert Holmes
DIRECTOR: David Maloney
STARS: Patrick Troughton, Frazer Hines, Wendy Padbury
ORIGINAL TRANSMISSION: 12/28/1968-1/18/1969

The Doctor and his companions intervene on behalf of the Gonds, who have been oppressed for centuries by aliens known as Krotons. The simplistic design of the titular terrors undermines an interesting story in which the unfortunate victims of tyranny are quite literally not intelligent enough to escape their ongoing captivity. Troughton and Padbury steal the show in the bit in which Zoe bests the Doctor in a test of individual intellectual prowess.

A. On what crystalline element are the Krotons based?

B. This is the first of how many *Doctor Who* serials to be written by prolific scribe Robert Holmes?

C. Gond students who pass the Krotons' test are ushered into what machine, which is actually the alien oppressors' downed spacecraft?

D. Who plays Beta, the Gond scientist who helps Jamie attack the Krotons' ship?

E. Frequent guest star Philip Madoc appeared in three episodes of what live-action Gerry Anderson science-fiction series in the early 1970s?

"The Seeds of Death"

WRITERS: Brian Hayles, Terrance Dicks
DIRECTOR: Michael Ferguson
STARS: Patrick Troughton, Frazer Hines, Wendy Padbury
ORIGINAL TRANSMISSION: 1/25-3/1/1969

The only problem with this tense, tightly paced return of the towering Ice Warriors is the basic set-up, which is a rehash of at least a half dozen other serials preceding it. Sinister Martians invade a transmat supply station on the moon, intent on using the teleportation device to facilitate an invasion of Earth. The hissing, heinous leader of the interloping aliens, Commander Slaar (brilliantly essayed by Alan Bennion), is one of the most memorable antagonists of the 1960s. This may have all been done before, but it's still a suspenseful good time.

A. Where do the Doctor and his companions first materialize in this serial?

B. What are the names of the Martian commanders portrayed by Alan Bennion in the two Third Doctor serials featuring the Ice Warriors?

C. How many Ice Warriors successfully reach Earth via the T-Mat?

D. Guest star Ronald Leigh-Hunt appears in what 1976 supernatural horror film, alongside Patrick Troughton?

E. Patrick Troughton does not appear in what episode of this serial?

"The Space Pirates"

WRITER: Robert Holmes
DIRECTOR: Michael Hart
STARS: Patrick Troughton, Frazer Hines, Wendy Padbury
ORIGINAL TRANSMISSION: 3/8-4/12/1969

In the program's purest foray into the space opera subgenre, the Doctor and his companions become embroiled in a conflict between cosmic police and plundering, interstellar pirates. Inventive and ambitious, this unusual adventure benefits greatly from a winning performance by guest star Gordon Gostelow, as an eccentric, rough-around-the-edges galactic pioneer. Though far from writer Holmes' best work, it's a nice change of pace from the "monster of the week" format.

A. How many navigational beacons are there in the galaxy's Fourth Sector?

B. Guest star Lisa Daniely co-starred with *Doctor Who* companion actress Deborah Watling in a late 1950s television series based on what H.G. Wells novel?

C. What is the name of Milo Clancey's well-traveled space ship?

D. "The Space Pirates" was the final serial produced by what prolific *Doctor Who* producer and former script editor?

E. Dudley Foster, who plays the villainous Caven in this serial, appeared in what 1969 Hammer cult science-fiction film alongside future *Doctor Who* villainess and *Space: 1999* star Catherine Schell?

"The War Games"

WRITERS: Malcolm Hulke, Terrance Dicks
DIRECTOR: David Maloney
STARS: Patrick Troughton, Frazer Hines, Wendy Padbury
ORIGINAL TRANSMISSION: 4/19-6/21/1969

In this glorious grand finale to the Troughton years, the Doctor and his companions thwart a group of would-be invaders who are abducting Earth soldiers from various historical periods and forcing them to fight a perpetual war, in order to create an invincible army. Nearly perfect in every facet of its production, this ten-part mega-epic is easily the finest curtain call for a departing Doctor and his companions to date. It's magnificent and monumental, a sweeping saga that's as historically significant as it is wholly thrilling.

A. What barrier separates the eleven time zones from each other?

B. "The War Games" features appearances by Patrick Troughton's oldest son, David, and Peter Craze, the younger brother of what former companion actor?

C. Guest star Clare Jenkins was hired to film just one scene for this story, reprising her role as Tanya Lernov from what Season Five serial?

D. What are the aliens' time-space machines called?

E. In defending his actions to the Time Lords, the Doctor refers to the Daleks, the Cybermen, the Yeti, the Ice Warriors, and what killer robots?

(Answers begin on Page 219.)

The Third Doctor

1970-1975, 1983

COMEDIC ACTOR JON PERTWEE PLAYED THE THIRD DOCTOR as a gadget-loving man of action, an aristocratic adventurer with the swashbuckling flair of D'Artagnan and the self-assured swagger of James Bond. Stripped of his knowledge of time travel and banished to Earth by the Time Lords, he still found plenty of adventure as the scientific advisor for U.N.I.T. (United Nations Intelligence Taskforce).

Pertwee came into the *Doctor Who* fold with an impressive resume of prior film and television credits, including scene-stealing roles in three of the popular *Carry On* films. A few years after leaving the series, Pertwee would again find small-screen success playing the popular children's character Worzel Gummidge. Jon Pertwee passed away in May of 1996, at the age of 76.

The Third Doctor met his on-screen fate when he absorbed a lethal dose of deadly cosmic radiation, after battling a giant spider on an alien world.

"Spearhead from Space"

WRITER: Robert Holmes
DIRECTOR: Derek Martinus
STARS: Jon Pertwee, Caroline John, Nicholas Courtney
ORIGINAL TRANSMISSION: 1/3-1/24/1970

The newly regenerated Doctor and U.N.I.T. battle murderous, living mannequins controlled by a malevolent alien force. Scenes of department store dummies smashing through storefronts and rampaging through the streets remain some of the most horrifying images in series' history. Pertwee strikes the perfect balance between aristocratic huffiness and comic eccentricity in his first outing, which also features strong turns by Courtney and John.

A. Liz Shaw (Caroline John) comes to U.N.I.T. from what prestigious university?

B. Caroline John is married to actor Geoffrey Beevers, who appears as the villainous Time Lord known as the Master in what Fourth Doctor serial?

C. The Third Doctor is shown to have what unusual mark on his forearm when he takes a shower in this story?

D. According to Channing (Hugh Burden), how long have the Nestenes been colonizing other worlds?

E. Guest star John Woodnutt appears as what villainous alien in "The Vanishing Earth," a 1973 episode of the cult science-fiction series *The Tomorrow People*?

"Doctor Who and the Silurians"

WRITER: Malcolm Hulke
DIRECTOR: Timothy Combe
STARS: Jon Pertwee, Caroline John, Nicholas Courtney
ORIGINAL TRANSMISSION: 1/31-3/14/1970

Prehistoric reptile men emerge from their underground dwellings and attempt to reclaim the surface world using a deadly virus. Taut and tense, this Quatermass-style offering works both as a straightforward science-fiction thriller and an allegory of real-world political tensions.

The Silurians have returned to *Doctor Who* on several occasions, but their debut story remains their best. This is the first of many 1970s serials to expertly exploit the eerie atmosphere of the rural English countryside.

A. What is the license plate number of the Doctor's vintage roadster Bessie?

B. The Silurians went into subterranean hibernation because they believed what object was going to crash into the Earth?

C. Guest star Geoffrey Palmer later appears as a treacherous starship captain in what Tenth Doctor story?

D. In the interim between his appearance here and his villainous guest turn in "Timelash," Paul Darrow was a regular on what Terry Nation-created science-fiction series?

E. The Silurians intend to destroy what protective field which surrounds the Earth, making the planet's atmosphere lethal to humans but perfect for them?

"The Ambassadors of Death"

WRITERS: David Whitaker, Trevor Ray, Malcolm Hulke
DIRECTOR: Michael Ferguson
STARS: Jon Pertwee, Caroline John, Nicholas Courtney
ORIGINAL TRANSMISSION: 3/21-5/2/1970

In this dark, extremely violent tale, radioactive alien beings come to Earth disguised as the astronauts of a doomed Mars probe. Lots of bloody gunplay and impressive stunt work keep the action moving along at a breakneck pace, but the real strength of the tale is the excellent performance of Pertwee, who once again finds his Doctor trying to mediate peace between aliens and humans seemingly bent on destroying one another.

A. What recurring character, played by John Levene, makes his first appearance in the series since "The Invasion" in the fifth episode of this serial?

B. The Doctor is attempting to repair what TARDIS component when he inadvertently sends Liz fifteen seconds into the future?

C. Guest star Michael Wisher made many *Doctor Who* appearances, but is best known for the Fourth Doctor serial "Genesis of the Daleks," in which he portrays what villainous scientist?

D. General Carrington (John Abineri) is the head of what newly formed division of the British space program?

E. What frequent *Doctor Who* guest star provides the voices for the alien ambassadors?

"Inferno"

WRITER: Don Houghton
DIRECTOR: Douglas Camfield
STARS: Jon Pertwee, Caroline John, Nicholas Courtney
ORIGINAL TRANSMISSION: 5/9-6/20/1970

An experimental drilling project uncovers a sinister force which turns anyone who comes into contact with it into a feral, primitive savage. Relentless tension propels this first-rate thriller, which also finds the Doctor traveling to a dystopian alternate dimension where his U.N.I.T. compatriots are ruthless Fascists. Courtney and John are frighteningly good as their Third Reich-inspired parallel reality counterparts.

A. Don Houghton went on to write the final three entries in a long-running Hammer film series featuring what legendary monster?

B. What alien martial art does the Doctor use to subdue Stahlman (Olaf Pooley)?

C. What is the name of the parallel Earth version of the United Nations Intelligence Taskforce?

D. Christopher Benjamin later appears as theater owner Henry Gordon Jago in what Fourth Doctor serial?

E. What common safety devices are used to paralyze the rampaging Primords during their attack on the parallel Earth control room?

"Terror of the Autons"

WRITER: Robert Holmes
DIRECTOR: Barry Letts
STARS: Jon Pertwee, Katy Manning, Nicholas Courtney
ORIGINAL TRANSMISSION: 1/2-1/23/1971

Roger Delgado takes *Doctor Who* villainy to a new level in his debut as the opportunistic Master. A rogue Time Lord conspires with the Nestene Consciousness to conquer the Earth, using living mannequins and acid-spraying plastic flowers. This colorful tale is a perfect blend of sinister scares and Saturday matinee adventure. Pertwee has a blast facing off against a worthy arch-enemy, and scenes of murderous troll dolls and man-eating plastic chairs are guaranteed to induce shivers.

A. This serial marks the first appearances of the Master, Jo Grant (Katy Manning), and what U.N.I.T. officer?

B. The Master steals the Nestene energy unit from what institution?

C. Guest star Harry Towb previously appeared in what Second Doctor serial?

D. The Master introduces himself to Rex Farrel (Michael Wisher) by what name?

E. The Doctor is attacked by what living plastic object at the end of Episode Three?

"The Mind of Evil"

WRITER: Don Houghton
DIRECTOR: Timothy Combe
STARS: Jon Pertwee, Katy Manning, Nicholas Courtney
ORIGINAL TRANSMISSION: 1/30-3/6/1971

In this James Bond-inspired entry, the Doctor must prevent the Master from using a mood-altering alien machine to spark a global war. The excellent prison setting, some rousing action sequences, and first-rate performances by the regulars are highlights of an enjoyable serial that sadly remains unreleased on DVD as a result of the failure of efforts to effectively colorize the only existing prints, which are in black and white.

A. Who plays Professor Emil Keller?

B. The alien parasite shows the Doctor images of a Dalek, a Cyberman, a Sensorite, a War Machine, a Zarbi, a Silurian, the Ice Lord Slaar, and what Season Two monster?

C. What weapon does the Master employ the prisoners of Stangmoor Prison to steal?

D. Guest star Michael Sheard went on to play an ill-fated Imperial Admiral in what *Star Wars* film?

E. Actress Pik-Sen Lim, who plays Captain Chin Lee, was married to what member of the production team for this serial until his death in 1991?

"The Claws of Axos"

WRITERS: Bob Baker, Dave Martin
DIRECTOR: Michael Ferguson
STARS: Jon Pertwee, Katy Manning, Nicholas Courtney
ORIGINAL TRANSMISSION: 3/13-4/3/1971

A massive, alien parasite which feeds on nuclear energy is lured to Earth by the Master. The hunt for the Doctor's devious nemesis continues in this atmospheric, visually striking entry. The monsters are well-designed and effectively realized, but the real fun comes in scenes where the frustrated Doctor makes no effort to mask his contempt for a stubborn government official determined to undermine U.N.I.T. at every turn.

A. Guest star Peter Bathurst played what character on the short-lived science-fiction series *Moonbase 3*, created by Barry Letts and Terrance Dicks?

B. What nuclear energy plant is the target of the power-hungry Axons?

C. Irritated by the Doctor's antiquated TARDIS, the Master says he might as well try and fly what common appliance?

D. Tim Pigott-Smith, who plays Captain Harker here, later appears in what 1976 Fourth Doctor serial?

E. "The Claws of Axos" is the first *Doctor Who* serial written by Bob Baker and Dave Martin, who would go on to create the villainous Omega and what iconic companion?

"The Colony in Space"

WRITER: Malcolm Hulke
DIRECTOR: Michael E. Briant
STARS: Jon Pertwee, Katy Manning, Nicholas Courtney
ORIGINAL TRANSMISSION: 4/10-5/15/1971

The first extraterrestrial outing for the Third Doctor is really just a rehash of the key ingredients of "The Mind of Evil," relocated to a remote alien setting. The Doctor and Jo travel to a distant planet, where settlers are being terrorized by giant reptiles. Though well-acted, the measured pacing works against a story that already feels a bit too familiar. One noteworthy element is the first appearance of the Time Lords since their debut in Patrick Troughton's final outing, "The War Games."

A. The Time Lords send the Doctor and Jo to what colonized planet?

B. The test firing of the Doomsday Weapon by the ancient denizens of the planet caused the creation of what cosmic body?

C. Morris Perry, who plays the ruthless Captain Dent here, appeared alongside frequent *Doctor Who* guest star John Woodnutt in what 1966 television short, which shares its name with the primary villain of this serial?

D. Dent and his thugs work for what company?

E. Guest star Tony Caunter's third and final appearance in the original series came in what Fifth Doctor serial?

"The Daemons"

WRITER: Guy Leopold
DIRECTOR: Christopher Barry
STARS: Jon Pertwee, Katy Manning, Nicholas Courtney
ORIGINAL TRANSMISSION: 5/22-6/19/1971

The supernatural horror craze of the early 1970s hits *Doctor Who* with this spooky, tightly paced tale of the Master summoning demon-like aliens to a tiny English village, in hopes of gaining their limitless power. Metaphysics and science-fiction blend remarkably well in this fan favorite, best remembered for the wonderful moment when the Brigadier points at a devilish creature and matter-of-factly orders, "Jenkins. Chap with wings, there. Five rounds rapid."

A. How far is the planet Damos from Earth?

B. The Master assumes what alias in this serial?

C. Two audio clips from this serial were used in what Tenth Doctor story?

D. "Guy Leopold" is a pseudonym for what two writers?

E. What is the license plate number of the Brigadier's car?

"Day of the Daleks"

WRITER: Louis Marks
DIRECTOR: Paul Bernard
STARS: Jon Pertwee, Katy Manning, Nicholas Courtney
ORIGINAL TRANSMISSION: 1/1-1/22/1972

More than a decade before *The Terminator* made Arnold Schwarzenegger a star, the Doctor battled time-traveling assassins in this rip-roaring science-fiction classic. Commandos from a dystopian future travel back to the twentieth century to eliminate the man they blame for facilitating a Dalek invasion of Earth. It's an exciting, action-packed tale of politics and paradoxes, enhanced by the debut of the Daleks' sadistic simian stormtroopers, the Ogrons.

A. What is the name of the diplomat the twenty-second-century rebels intend to assassinate?

B. Guest star Anna Barry, who plays the rebel leader Anat, went on to appear with more conventional doctors in the first episode of what 1970s British soap opera, which shares its title and setting with a long-running American daytime drama?

C. What fictional principle, which prohibits a time traveler from interfering with his or her own past actions, is first cited by the Doctor in this serial?

D. "Day of the Daleks" is the first serial since "Inferno" not to feature what recurring character?

E. Guest star Scott Fredericks later appears in what Fourth Doctor serial?

"The Curse of Peladon"

WRITER: Brian Hayles
DIRECTOR: Lenny Mayne
STARS: Jon Pertwee, Katy Manning
ORIGINAL TRANSMISSION: 1/29-2/19/1972

The Doctor and Jo investigate murder and treachery at a summit to determine whether the planet Peladon will join the Galactic Federation. Set-bound but immensely enjoyable, this tale of intrigue and espionage marks a fine return for one of the most memorable alien adversaries of the Patrick Troughton era. Troughton's own son, David, delivers a memorable guest turn as a king torn between tradition and the desire for progress, and hopelessly smitten with Manning's Jo.

A. What is the name of the ancient beast which haunts the Citadel?

B. The hermaphroditic hexapod Alpha Centauri is played by what two thespians?

C. Guest star Geoffrey Toone portrayed what character in the 1965 theatrical film *Doctor Who and the Daleks*, originally played in the serial "The Daleks" by Alan Wheatley?

D. The electronic key found by Jo is composed of what Martian ore?

E. David Troughton later appears as Professor Hobbes in what claustrophobic Tenth Doctor story?

"The Sea Devils"

WRITER: Malcolm Hulke
DIRECTOR: Michael E. Briant
STARS: Jon Pertwee, Katy Manning
ORIGINAL TRANSMISSION: 2/26-4/1/1972

It's breathless action on the high seas in this gripping, suspenseful tale of aquatic cousins of the Silurians laying siege to British naval bases, with the help of the Master. The cooperation of the Royal Navy ensured both a high degree of authenticity and a sweeping sense of adventure, making this one of the most pulse-pounding, edge-of-your-seat entries of the decade. Delgado and Pertwee are fabulous in a prolonged and well-choreographed sword duel.

A. What does the Doctor say the creatures previously designated as Silurians should have been called?

B. Clive Morton, who plays Trenchard, appeared in what 1961 crime thriller with future *Doctor Who* guest stars Honor Blackman and Richard Briers?

C. Prior to having his character replaced by a CG effect for the Special Edition, guest star Declan Mulholland played what slimy villain in a deleted scene from the original *Star Wars*?

D. The Sea Devils raid what Royal Navy base?

E. The Master watches what long-running children's television series in his prison cell?

"The Mutants"

WRITERS: Bob Baker, Dave Martin
DIRECTOR: Christopher Barry
STARS: Jon Pertwee, Katy Manning
ORIGINAL TRANSMISSION: 4/8-5/13/1972

The Doctor and Jo contend with a power-hungry military officer and mutant insect-men on the Earth colony of Solos. This brilliantly acted six-part serial is one of Pertwee's best. The mutant monsters look great, the cliffhangers are truly harrowing, and Paul Whitsun-Jones' sadistic Marshall is an absolutely magnificent villain. Pay close attention and you'll work out the secret of the Solonian mutants before the Doctor does, but that won't diminish the action or suspense in the least.

A. How long does it take for the planet Solos to circle its sun?

B. Guest star Geoffrey Palmer was a regular on what short-lived BBC sitcom which was created by "Amy's Choice" writer Simon Nye, and shares its title with a First Doctor serial?

C. A mutant "Mutt" appears briefly in what Fourth Doctor serial, also directed by Christopher Barry?

D. Who is the intended recipient of the message given to the Doctor by the Time Lords?

E. This was the final serial scored by composer Tristram Cary, who also wrote music for the Hammer's *Blood from the Mummy's Tomb* and what Nigel Kneale-scripted science-fiction thriller?

"The Time Monster"

WRITERS: Robert Sloman, Barry Letts
DIRECTOR: Paul Bernard
STARS: Jon Pertwee, Katy Manning, Nicholas Courtney
ORIGINAL TRANSMISSION: 5/20-6/24/1972

The Master is at it again, this time posing as a research scientist in order to build a machine that will allow him to harness the power of a terrible monster from lost Atlantis. This weird, wild outing is perhaps the most libidinous of the classic series, loaded with innuendo, double entendre, and the ample cleavage of late Hammer horror queen Ingrid Pitt. In one typically amusing scene, the Doctor and the Master have a brief discussion about poor Jo's bruised backside.

A. Ingrid Pitt appears in what Fifth Doctor serial, also set on the ocean floor?

B. What does the acronym TOMTIT stand for?

C. Guest star David Prowse, best known for playing Darth Vader in the original *Star Wars* trilogy, essayed the Frankenstein monster in the 1966 film version of *Casino Royale* and which two Hammer horror films?

D. Which recurring character is reduced to an infant by the TOMTIT machine?

E. Kronos is actually what type of destructive creature?

"The Three Doctors"

WRITERS: Bob Baker, Dave Martin
DIRECTOR: Lenny Mayne
STARS: Jon Pertwee, Patrick Troughton, William Hartnell, Katy Manning, Nicholas Courtney
ORIGINAL TRANSMISSION: 12/30-1/20/1973

The Time Lords call upon the first three incarnations of the Doctor to stop the vengeful Omega, who is draining energy from their world in an attempt to escape imprisonment inside a black hole. The dimension-hopping narrative is exciting enough, but the lively, antagonistic interplay between Pertwee and Troughton is the real draw. Hartnell, who was ill during production, makes a minimal but quite memorable contribution.

A. Lenny Mayne was married to what actress, who appeared in minor roles in "The Monster of Peladon" and "The Hand of Fear," until his death in 1977?

B. In exchange for his help in defeating Omega (Stephen Thorne), the Time Lords restore the Doctor's knowledge of time travel and replace what component of his TARDIS?

C. Guest star Clyde Pollitt, who plays the Chancellor here, also portrayed a Time Lord in what earlier serial?

D. What object does the Second Doctor misplace in the TARDIS?

E. Omega's alternate universe is composed of what?

"Carnival of Monsters"

WRITER: Robert Holmes
DIRECTOR: Barry Letts
STARS: Jon Pertwee, Katy Manning
ORIGINAL TRANSMISSION: 1/27-2/17/1973

The series' transition from Earth-bound action to cosmic fantasy begins in earnest with this funny, fast-paced adventure in which the Doctor and Jo find themselves trapped in a miniaturized zoo with a host of deadly alien monsters. The enormous, serpentine Drashigs are among the best *Doctor Who* creatures of the 1970s, and are long overdue for a return. Fans of the Fourth Doctor era should keep an eye out for a familiar face aboard the *S.S. Bernice.*

A. What illegal machine is home to the menagerie of alien monsters?

B. Guest star Tenniel Evans, a longtime co-star of Jon Pertwee in the radio series *The Navy Lark*, took over a role created by Patrick Troughton in what TV sitcom when the Second Doctor actor died in 1987?

C. The calendar on the bulkhead of the *SS Bernice* indicates it is what year?

D. The Doctor claims to have taken boxing lessons from what legendary heavyweight champion?

E. Leslie Dwyer appeared in several installments of the long-running cop drama *Z Cars*, including what 1962 episode featuring future *Doctor Who* villain Roger Delgado?

"Frontier in Space"

WRITER: Malcolm Hulke
DIRECTORS: Paul Bernard, David Maloney
STARS: Jon Pertwee, Katy Manning
ORIGINAL TRANSMISSION: 2/24-3/31/1973

It's pre-*Star Wars* space opera at its small-screen best in this sweeping tale of brinkmanship on the edge of the galaxy. The Master employs the brutish Ogrons to help spark an intergalactic war between humans and the lizard-like Draconians. Though much of the story involves the Doctor and Jo being incarcerated in one cell after another, this one still moves along at a breakneck pace, and features stellar performances by Pertwee, Manning, and Roger Delgado.

A. Humans refer to the Draconians by what derogatory name?

B. This serial marks the final appearance for what frequent guest star, who was killed in a car crash a few months after its initial broadcast?

C. Guest star Luan Peters previously appeared in the Second Doctor serial "The Macra Terror" under what stage name?

D. The Doctor and Jo are accused of being spies and career criminals from what planet?

E. The Master is shown reading what classic science-fiction novel by H.G. Wells?

"Planet of the Daleks"

WRITER: Terry Nation
DIRECTOR: David Maloney
STARS: Jon Pertwee, Katy Manning
ORIGINAL TRANSMISSION: 4/7-5/12/1973

The Doctor, Jo, and a group of Thals battle a deadly virus and invisible Daleks on the jungle planet of Spiridon in this tense, thoroughly thrilling offering. Danger lurks at every turn as the story progresses, making this that rare *Doctor Who* serial in which the viewer wonders if the Time Lord and his trusty companion will survive until the closing credits of the final episode. It's a fitting follow-up to the fabulous "Frontier in Space," made even more enjoyable by fine performances from frequent guest stars Bernard Horsfall and Prentis Hancock.

A. Hilary Minister, who plays Marat in this story, appears as an unnamed Thal in what other *Doctor Who* serial?

B. The TARDIS becomes encased in what organic substance, trapping the Doctor inside as the emergency oxygen supply runs out?

C. The Doctor and his friends hide from the Dalek patrol in what rocky region of Spiridon?

D. Guest star Tim Preece went on to appear in "War Games," a 2002 episode of what period detective series?

E. The core of Spiridon is composed of a magma-like allotrope of what?

"The Green Death"

WRITERS: Robert Sloman, Barry Letts
DIRECTOR: Michael E. Briant
STARS: Jon Pertwee, Katy Manning, Nicholas Courtney
ORIGINAL TRANSMISSION: 5/19-6/23/1973

Younger fans accustomed to the tearful farewells exchanged by the Tenth Doctor and his companions will feel right at home in the closing moments of this, Manning's final original series outing as the ditzy but endearing Jo Grant. Prior to the moving denouement, this story of giant maggots terrorizing miners near a wasteful chemical plant is an expert exercise in skin-crawling environmental horror. Guest star Stewart Bevan develops a nice chemistry with Manning as the story unfolds, facilitating one of the most credible departures for a longtime assistant in series' history.

A. What rather derogatory nickname do the locals give the environmentally-conscious commune run by Professor Clifford Jones (Stewart Bevan)?

B. The Doctor visits what alien world in this serial?

C. Guest star Mitzi McKenzie went on to appear in the 1984 big-screen adaptation of what classic science-fiction novel about a dystopian future?

D. Jerome Willis, who plays Stevens here, appeared as the maniacal Professor Nero in several episodes of what early 1970s children's action series, opposite former *Doctor Who* star Wendy Padbury?

E. What does the acronym BOSS stand for?

"The Time Warrior"

WRITER: Robert Holmes
DIRECTOR: Alan Bromly
STARS: Jon Pertwee, Elisabeth Sladen, Nicholas Courtney
ORIGINAL TRANSMISSION: 12/15/1973-1/5/1974

Guest players Kevin Lindsay and David Daker engage in a spirited battle for the spotlight in this immensely enjoyable tale of a militaristic alien snatching human scientists back through time to help him repair his damaged spacecraft. The only historical tale of the Pertwee era introduces several elements which continue to influence *Doctor Who* to this day, including beloved companion Sarah Jane Smith (Sladen) and the stout, sadistic Sontarans.

A. This serial features the first mention of the name of what very important alien world?

B. David Daker went on to appear in what 1981 comedic fantasy about a young boy and a band of dwarfs traveling through time and space to steal valuable artifacts?

C. What is the first name of Sarah Jane Smith's aunt?

D. Guest star Alan Rowe later appears in what Fourth Doctor serial in which the Time Lord faces off against a Rutan, a mortal enemy of the Sontarans?

E. Linx (Kevin Lindsay) uses what device to travel through time and kidnap twentieth-century scientists?

"Invasion of the Dinosaurs"

WRITER: Malcolm Hulke
DIRECTOR: Paddy Russell
STARS: Jon Pertwee, Elisabeth Sladen, Nicholas Courtney
ORIGINAL TRANSMISSION: 1/12-2/16/1974

Execution doesn't quite live up to ambition in this effects-laden outing in which a secret cabal of environmental scientists attempts to undo the damage done to the Earth by man with the help of a horde of prehistoric reptiles. Though well-paced and action-packed, some of the dinosaur props just don't hold up very well. One intriguing element is the treason of U.N.I.T. Captain Mike Yates, the first instance of a longtime friend of the Doctor becoming an enemy.

A. What is the license plate number of the Whomobile, the Doctor's new car?

B. What is the first type of dinosaur encountered by the Doctor and Sarah?

C. What actor, best known for portraying Georgie in the film version of Anthony Burgess' *A Clockwork Orange*, plays the thirteenth-century peasant who appears in modern London?

D. Guest star Carmen Silvera previously appeared in multiple roles in what First Doctor serial?

E. Butler (Martin Jarvis) and the other conspirators give their plan what optimistic name?

"Death to the Daleks"

WRITER: Terry Nation
DIRECTOR: Michael E. Briant
STARS: Jon Pertwee, Elisabeth Sladen
ORIGINAL TRANSMISSION: 2/23-3/16/1974

The Doctor and Sarah aid enslaved natives and a crew of shipwrecked humans against the Daleks on the planet Exxilon, where a mysterious structure drains away all electrical energy. The last Dalek outing of the Pertwee era is solid but not spectacular, highlights including the first instance of a companion wearing a two-piece bathing suit, and the antagonists' clever conversion of their powerless weapons into old-fashioned machine guns.

A. According to the Doctor, the Daleks use what force to move around in this story?

B. What precious mineral is readily available only on the planet Exxilon?

C. Guest star Duncan Lamont appeared in what groundbreaking 1953 BBC mini-series which was remade (with David Tennant) in 2005, and heavily influenced the format of *Doctor Who*?

D. John Abineri, who plays Richard Ralton here, was a regular on what mid-1970s science-fiction series created by Terry Nation?

E. Where does the Doctor say he's seen the markings on the walls of the Exxilon City before?

"The Monster of Peladon"

WRITER: Brian Hayles
DIRECTOR: Lenny Mayne
STARS: Jon Pertwee, Elisabeth Sladen
ORIGINAL TRANSMISSION: 3/23-4/27/1974

The Doctor returns to Peladon, where he and Sarah become embroiled in a murderous plot by Martian conspirators to steal the planet's most valuable element. Though basically a protracted rehash of the previous Peladon story, the penultimate outing for Pertwee is still suspenseful and quite satisfying. This slick six-parter marks the final appearance of the green-skinned, reptilian men from Mars to date.

A. Though he is listed only as "Miner" in the credits, guest star Roy Evans' character is given what name in the dialogue?

B. This serial marks the first and only time the Martians refer to themselves by what commonly used name?

C. The Galactic Federation is at war with the forces of what cosmic confederacy?

D. Guest star Graeme Eton later appears as an ill-fated lighthouse keeper in what Fourth Doctor serial?

E. What unusual alien from "The Curse of Peladon" returns in this serial, now acting as a Federation Ambassador to the planet?

"Planet of the Spiders"

WRITERS: Robert Sloman, Barry Letts
DIRECTOR: Barry Letts
STARS: Jon Pertwee, Elisabeth Sladen, Nicholas Courtney
ORIGINAL TRANSMISSION: 5/4-6/8/1974

The Third Doctor's run comes to a rather uneven end in this exciting but overlong tale of alien arachnids from the oft-referenced planet of Metebelis 3. The best elements are the hideous mammoth spiders, the redemption of Mike Yates, and the stellar performance of Pertwee. Unfortunately, the tale is padded with a protracted chase scene that takes up nearly an entire episode and does little to further the plot. The Brigadier's reaction to the climactic regeneration is absolutely priceless.

A. "Planet of the Spiders" replaced what proposed story as the Third Doctor's curtain call when actor Roger Delgado was killed in an automobile accident?

B. Guest star Carl Forgione went on to appear as a Neanderthal in what Seventh Doctor serial?

C. What does Lupton steal from the Doctor's laboratory at U.N.I.T. headquarters?

D. Guest star Jenny Laird previously appeared alongside two-time *Doctor Who* guest star Bernard Archard in the 1960 film adaptation of what chilling John Wyndham novel?

E. K'anpo Rinpoche (George Cormack), the elderly Abbot of the monastery, is actually what type of alien being?

(Answers begin on Page 223.)

The Fourth Doctor

1974-1981

A TRUE ECCENTRIC OFF-CAMERA, TOM BAKER BROUGHT a seemingly boundless energy to the role of the Doctor, transforming him from a slightly aloof aristocrat to an unpredictable, Bohemian madman. With his bombastic voice, Cheshire cat grin, and larger-than-life personality, Baker could credibly transition from childish silliness to somber contemplation to righteous indignation and back again all in the same breath. His scenery-chewing, improvisational approach to the part proved wildly popular with audiences of all ages, all over the world.

Baker was a struggling actor in 1974, winning the role largely on the strength of his bravura turn as the villainous sorcerer Koura in that year's *The Golden Voyage of Sinbad.* By the time he left the series seven seasons later, his battered hat, wide smile, curly locks, and long, multi-colored scarf had become as closely identified with the Doctor as a bullwhip and fedora are with Indiana Jones today.

The Fourth Doctor's tenure ended when he fell from a radio telescope tower after thwarting an evil scheme hatched by his arch-enemy, the Master (Anthony Ainley).

"Robot"

WRITER: Terrance Dicks
DIRECTOR: Christopher Barry
STARS: Tom Baker, Elisabeth Sladen, Ian Marter, Nicholas Courtney
ORIGINAL TRANSMISSION: 12/28/1974-1/18/1975

The newly regenerated Doctor helps U.N.I.T. battle a giant robot employed by a cabal of geniuses plotting to impose a new world order. Baker slips effortlessly into the starring role in this expertly crafted, thoroughly enjoyable science-fiction reworking of *King Kong*. Sladen and Marter are excellent, and the climactic battle between the military and the gargantuan mechanical monster harkens back to the "monster on the loose" epics of the 1950s.

A. What is the name of the Think Tank scientist who developed the titular robot K1?

B. Though he didn't appear on-screen until the first episode of this story, Ian Marter's Harry Sullivan is first mentioned in what Third Doctor serial?

C. Who plays Think Tank director Hilda Winters?

D. Among the items in the Doctor's pockets is an honorary membership to what interstellar athletic organization?

E. In addition to playing the robot here and the Cyber Controller in two serials, towering actor Michael Kilgarriff appears as an ape-like Ogron in what Third Doctor story?

"The Ark in Space"

WRITERS: Robert Holmes, John Lucarotti
DIRECTOR: Rodney Bennett
STARS: Tom Baker, Elisabeth Sladen, Ian Marter
ORIGINAL TRANSMISSION: 1/25-2/15/1975

Wasp-like aliens and their slimy larva overtake a space station manned by the survivors of a thirtieth-century Earth disaster in this creepy, well-acted potboiler. The brilliant Nerva ark sets are among the best ever constructed for a television program, giving this one a cinematic quality. Though the adult Wirrn are not as well realized as other technical aspects of this first-rate production, their first appearance on-screen remains one of the most effective shock shots of the classic series.

A. Who does the Doctor say knitted his trademark scarf for him?

B. Prior to taking up residence in "The Ark in Space," guest star Wendy Williams appeared in what 1960 episode of the iconic spy series *Danger Man*?

C. The Doctor uses what common device to take a gravity reading aboard the Nerva ark?

D. What is the real name of the ark crewmember nicknamed Noah (played by Kenton Moore)?

E. Guest star John Gregg, who plays the ill-fated Lycett here, later appears in "The Choice," a 2001 episode of what Rockne S. O'Bannon-created science-fiction series?

"The Sontaran Experiment"

WRITERS: Bob Baker, Dave Martin
DIRECTOR: Rodney Bennett
STARS: Tom Baker, Elisabeth Sladen, Ian Marter
ORIGINAL TRANSMISSION: 2/22-3/1/1975

The return of the potato-headed warmongers first introduced in the Third Doctor classic "The Time Warrior" is a truncated triumph, fueled by fine performances all around. The Doctor and his companions are transported to Earth, where a Sontaran scout subjects helpless humans to horrible scientific tests. Thrifty but undeniably thrilling, this budget-minded outing is a testament to the boundless ingenuity of the production team of the period.

A. Guest star Terry Walsh, who plays the astronaut Zake, also doubled for which regular cast member who suffered a broken collarbone during filming?

B. How do the Doctor and his companions get to Earth from Space Station Nerva?

C. Who plays the Sontaran Marshal that Field Major Styre (Kevin Lindsay) communicates with via cosmic video link?

D. Harry removes what vital component from Styre's ship?

E. Sarah Jane Smith reunites with retired U.N.I.T. officer Alistair Gordon Lethbridge-Stewart to battle a vengeful Sontaran in what story on *The Sarah Jane Adventures*?

"Genesis of the Daleks"

WRITER: Terry Nation
DIRECTOR: David Maloney
STARS: Tom Baker, Elisabeth Sladen, Ian Marter
ORIGINAL TRANSMISSION: 3/8-4/12/1975

The Time Lords send the Doctor and his companions to Skaro in the distant past, where they are charged with preventing the creation of the Daleks. This extremely bleak but exceptionally brilliant epic is, without doubt, the most important and influential *Doctor Who* serial since "The Dalek Invasion of Earth." Michael Wisher's magnificent Davros is a villain for the ages, a being so sinister and single-minded that he actually manages to steal scenes from the flamboyant Baker.

A. Before appearing as Davros' right-hand man Nyder here, Peter Miles helped engineer an Earth invasion of sorts in what Third Doctor serial?

B. What device do the Time Lords give to the Doctor to facilitate his escape from Skaro?

C. Guy Siner went on to co-star with two-time *Doctor Who* guest actress Carmen Silvera in *'Allo 'Allo!*, and appears as the father of what regular crewmember in an episode of *Star Trek: Enterprise*?

D. Who betrays the Kaleds by giving the Thals chemicals that will weaken the walls of the Kaled dome?

E. Davros originally refers to his creation by what innocuous-sounding name?

"Revenge of the Cybermen"

WRITER: Gerry Davis
DIRECTOR: Michael E. Briant
STARS: Tom Baker, Elisabeth Sladen, Ian Marter
ORIGINAL TRANSMISSION: 4/19-5/10/1975

The Doctor, Harry, and Sarah attempt to stop the Cybermen from destroying the gold planet Voga. An oft-maligned outing which suffers primarily from comparisons to the legendary tale it follows; this one still has a lot going for it. The beautiful Nerva station sets are back, Sladen and Marter have fun bantering back and forth, and Christopher Robbie's Cyber Leader is a classic pulp antagonist. Though a weak final chapter of a very strong season, it's still a highly entertaining bit of space opera.

A. What planetary transport is re-routed away from the Nerva Beacon due to quarantine in the story's opening moments?

B. What was the original name of the planet Voga?

C. What weapon did humans invent to defeat the Cybermen in the Cyber war?

D. Christopher Robbie previously appeared as a costumed do-gooder in what Second Doctor serial?

E. What supposedly cursed Somerset tourist attraction provided the primary exterior location for this serial?

"Terror of the Zygons"

WRITER: Robert Banks Stewart
DIRECTOR: Douglas Camfield
STARS: Tom Baker, Elisabeth Sladen, Ian Marter, Nicholas Courtney
ORIGINAL TRANSMISSION: 8/30-9/20/1975

The Doctor and his companions investigate the destruction of offshore oil rigs and encounter the Loch Ness monster in contemporary Scotland. This immensely entertaining blend of horror, mystery, and giant monster mayhem is one of the best serials of the Fourth Doctor era. Colorful supporting characters, unforgettable aliens, and winning performances from the leads (especially the departing Marter) add up to a true classic.

A. What Sixth Doctor serial provides an alternate explanation of the true nature of the Loch Ness monster?

B. Guest star Robert Russell, who plays the Caber, previously appeared as a guard in what Second Doctor serial?

C. The Duke of Forgill (John Woodnutt) is the president of what governmental organization?

D. Sarah is attacked by a Zygon disguised as what U.N.I.T. officer?

E. "Terror of the Zygons" marks the final *Doctor Who* appearance of what popular supporting actor until "Mawdryn Undead" in 1983?

"Planet of Evil"

WRITER: Louis Marks
DIRECTOR: David Maloney
STARS: Tom Baker, Elisabeth Sladen
ORIGINAL TRANSMISSION: 9/27-10/18/1975

In this tense and well-essayed adventure, the Doctor and Sarah are menaced by antimatter monsters aboard a ship being drawn inexorably toward its doom. Of particular note is Prentis Hancock's wonderful, scenery-chewing turn as the unbalanced Salamar. Most of the hallmarks of the Phillip Hinchcliffe era are on display, from graphic violence and a grim tone to the flagrant "borrowing" of classic literary and film plots, and the familiar recipe adds up to a very palatable confection. The lavish sets are nothing short of breathtaking.

A. The 1956 film *Forbidden Planet*, which heavily influenced this serial, was itself based on what seventeenth-century William Shakespeare play?

B. Which two Shakespeare plays are quoted by the Doctor in this story?

C. The ill-fated geological expedition headed by Professor Sorenson (Frederick Jaeger) came to Zeta Minor from what planet?

D. Guest star Louis Mahoney later appears in what frightening Tenth Doctor story?

E. What member of the crew refuses Salamar's command to eject Sarah and the Doctor into space?

"Pyramids of Mars"

WRITER: Stephen Harris
DIRECTOR: Paddy Russell
STARS: Tom Baker, Elisabeth Sladen
ORIGINAL TRANSMISSION: 10/25-11/15/1975

The Doctor and Sarah encounter robotic mummies and an all-powerful alien entity in this gripping gothic chiller. The easy chemistry between Baker and Sladen gives way to some of the finest performances and sharpest dialogue exchanges of the season, and even leads to some improvised, tension-breaking slapstick in the final episode. Though the mummies don't really work, the vainglorious Sutekh (Gabriel Woolf) is a perfect adversary for the larger-than-life Fourth Doctor.

A. What year does Sarah say she is from in this serial?

B. Stephen Harris is a pseudonym for Robert Holmes and what writer, who previously helped create the game show *Whodunnit?* for BBC TV?

C. In addition to Horus, how many gods are named on the tomb of Thutmosis III?

D. What unusual aspect of the Doctor's physiology allows him to survive being strangled by a robotic mummy?

E. Guest star Michael Bilton previously appeared in "The Massacre of St. Bartholomew's Eve," and went on to play a Time Lord in what later Fourth Doctor serial?

"The Android Invasion"

WRITER: Terry Nation
DIRECTOR: Barry Letts
STARS: Tom Baker, Elisabeth Sladen, Ian Marter
ORIGINAL TRANSMISSION: 11/22-12/13/1975

The Doctor and Sarah land in a village near a U.N.I.T. base, only to discover that its residents are frighteningly realistic androids. The only real disappointment in this creepy, *Avengers*-style offering is the glaring absence of Nicolas Courtney's Brigadier Lethbridge-Stewart. Otherwise, it's a fine outing, showcasing excellent villains, more great interplay between Baker and Sladen, and the final *Doctor Who* appearances of Ian Marter and John Levene.

A. What drink does the Doctor order in the pub in Devesham?

B. Guest star Patrick Newell played what recurring character in the final season of *The Avengers*?

C. What article of clothing worn by the android Sarah alerts the Doctor that she's not the real Sarah Jane Smith?

D. Where does Guy Crayford (Milton Johns) say the Brigadier has gone to, leaving Colonel Faraday (Patrick Newell) in charge of the Space Defense Station?

E. Peter Welch, who plays Morgan here, previously appeared as a British soldier in what Second Doctor serial?

"The Brain of Morbius"

WRITER: Robin Bland
DIRECTOR: Christopher Barry
STARS: Tom Baker, Elisabeth Sladen
ORIGINAL TRANSMISSION: 1/3-1/24/1976

No actor has ever played a *Doctor Who* villain with the intensity or relish of Philip Madoc, and this superlative science-fiction updating of Mary Shelley's *Frankenstein* showcases him at his sinister best. The brain of a renegade Time Lord has been preserved by an ambitious scientist, who is building a new body for it from corpses recovered from wrecked spacecraft. This mad, macabre outing is popcorn entertainment of the highest order.

A. Condo (Colin Fay) wants Solon (Philip Madoc) to surgically replace what?

B. Guest star Michael Spice, who provides the voice of Morbius in this serial, also lends his vocal talents to the villainous Magnus Greel in what later Fourth Doctor adventure?

C. The members of the Sisterhood of Karn believe that the Doctor has been sent by the Time Lords to steal the last of what liquid?

D. What type of gas does the Doctor pipe into Solon's operating room?

E. Robin Bland is a pseudonym for what two writers?

"The Seeds of Doom"

WRITER: Robert Banks Stewart
DIRECTOR: Douglas Camfield
STARS: Tom Baker, Elisabeth Sladen
ORIGINAL TRANSMISSION: 1/31-3/6/1976

World class villainy and spine-tingling thrills grow on trees in this terrifying tale of deadly plants from outer space. Tony Beckley is magnificent as the plant-obsessed Harrison Chase, John Challis menacing as the mercenary Scorby, and Sylvia Coleridge irresistible as the rather batty Amelia Ducat. Scenes of unfortunate souls slowly transformed into vicious, ambulatory vegetables will make you shiver, and the gruesome climax in the compost machine may make you swear off salad forever.

A. Sir Colin Thackeray (Michael Barrington) is in charge of what environmental agency?

B. What Welsh actor, who previously appeared in "Fury from the Deep" and "The War Games," makes his final *Doctor Who* guest appearance in this serial, playing an ill-fated botanist?

C. What U.N.I.T. officer leads the assault on the Krynoids on Harrison Chase's estate?

D. Guest star John Gleeson went on to appear as a Doctor in "Fluff Daddy," a 2001 episode of what adult-oriented science-fiction series?

E. The Doctor claims to be the president of what cosmic botanical organization?

"The Masque of Mandragora"

WRITER: Louis Marks
DIRECTOR: Rodney Bennett
STARS: Tom Baker, Elisabeth Sladen
ORIGINAL TRANSMISSION: 9/4-9/25/1976

Malevolent living energy from beyond the stars exerts its evil influence over the members of an ancient cult in fifteenth-century Italy. Though not quite as effective or memorable as the previous season's best efforts, this fun historical outing does feature some excellent location work at the Polmeirion tourist resort in North Wales and spirited performances from the leads and guest players alike. Of particular note is Tim Pigott-Smith as the fiercely loyal Marco.

A. Who does the Doctor tell Giuliano was the finest swordsman he's ever known?

B. Tim Pigott-Smith appears as the British Foreign Secretary in what installment of the long-running James Bond film series?

C. Rodney Bennett directed what 1980 television adaptation of an iconic Shakespeare play, starring *Doctor Who* luminaries Lalla Ward, Claire Bloom, Geoffrey Beevers, and Derek Jacobi?

D. In what Ninth Doctor story does the Doctor explain the true nature of the "Time Lord gift" (a telepathic field, generated by the TARDIS) which here allows Sarah to understand fifteenth-century Italian?

E. Hieronymous (Norman Jones) is the leader of what ancient, forbidden order?

"The Hand of Fear"

WRITERS: Bob Baker, Dave Martin
DIRECTOR: Lenny Mayne
STARS: Tom Baker, Elisabeth Sladen
ORIGINAL TRANSMISSION: 10/2-10/23/1976

Sladen gets a memorable send-off in a tale in which the Doctor's longtime companion is possessed by the fossil of a severed alien hand and nearly causes a catastrophic nuclear meltdown. From her garish Andy Pandy overalls to her wistful farewell scene, this one is Sarah Jane Smith's show throughout. The suspenseful story's oft-repeated catch-phrase "Eldrad must live!" is guaranteed to be stuck in your head long after the closing credits roll.

A. The treacherous Eldrad is from what planet?

B. What two thespians portray Eldrad?

C. Guest star Glyn Houston, who plays Professor Watson here, later appears as a military officer in what Fifth Doctor serial?

D. Sarah whistles what tune, written by Joseph Tabrar in 1892, as she departs for home?

E. After leaving the original *Doctor Who*, Elisabeth Sladen first reprised her role as Sarah Jane Smith in "A Girl's Best Friend," the pilot episode of what proposed spin-off series?

"The Deadly Assassin"

WRITER: Robert Holmes
DIRECTOR: David Maloney
STAR: Tom Baker
ORIGINAL TRANSMISSION: 10/30-11/20/1976

The Doctor is accused of assassinating the Lord High President of Gallifrey (Llewellyn Rees), and must declare himself a candidate for the office in order to stay his execution and prove his innocence. This lively, violent cosmic take on *The Manchurian Candidate* is both a perfect show-case for the talented Baker and a first-rate political thriller. Most of what we know about the Doctor's people and home planet was introduced in this classic serial, the first ever to feature no regular companion.

A. Who was the Doctor's teacher at Prydon Academy?

B. This serial features the first mention of the legendary Time Lord Rassilon, who later appears as a villainous madman in what Tenth Doctor story?

C. How many actors played Borusa throughout his numerous appearances in the original *Doctor Who*?

D. Chancellor Goth (Bernard Horsfall) claims to have found the ailing Master on what planet?

E. Guest star Eric Chitty previously appeared as apothecary Charles Preslin in the first episode of what First Doctor historical adventure?

"The Face of Evil"

WRITER: Chris Boucher
DIRECTOR: Pennant Roberts
STARS: Tom Baker, Louise Jameson
ORIGINAL TRANSMISSION: 1/1-1/22/1977

On a jungle planet, a savage tribe wages a fruitless war to free a mysterious god from the priest-like people they believe are holding the deity hostage. The fierce Leela is that rare post-feminist fantasy heroine who strikes a perfect balance between sexuality and self-reliance, and Jameson is magnificent in the role. The sight of the god Xoanon's frighteningly familiar face carved into the side of a mountain is one of the series' all-time great reveals.

A. What lethal flora do the warriors of the Sevateem use to dispatch their enemies?

B. Guest star Leslie Schofield has an uncredited role as Chief Bast in what infamous television special, based on a classic science-fiction film?

C. The Doctor must take what deadly test to prove he's not the Evil One?

D. Guest star Leon Eagles went on to appear in "Carrier Pigeons," a 1987 episode of what action series about a trio of female private detectives?

E. The Doctor claims to have been taught how to fire a crossbow by what famous archer?

"The Robots of Death"

WRITER: Chris Boucher
DIRECTOR: Michael E. Briant
STARS: Tom Baker, Louise Jameson
ORIGINAL TRANSMISSION: 1/29-2/19/1977

It's Agatha Christie's *Ten Little Indians* in space as the Doctor and Leela investigate the violent deaths of several humans aboard a mining ship staffed with sinister-looking mechanical men. Stellar performances and escalating tension make this Isaac Asimov-influenced outing an edge-of-your-seat success. There's also a fair amount of effective social commentary here, the human crewmembers of Storm Mine 4 having grown apathetic and largely ineffectual due to an increasing reliance on technology.

A. What medical term does the Doctor use to describe robophobia, the irrational fear of robots?

B. Guest star Pamela Salem played Miss Moneypenny in what 1983 remake of the James Bond thriller *Thunderball*?

C. Which robot aboard the Storm Mine 4 is actually an undercover security operative for the mining company that owns the vessel?

D. Who is the first member of the Storm Mine 4 crew to be found dead?

E. David Bailie, who portrays Dask here, appears as what minor character in the first three *Pirates of the Caribbean* films?

"The Talons of Weng-Chiang"

WRITER: Robert Holmes
DIRECTOR: David Maloney
STARS: Tom Baker, Louise Jameson
ORIGINAL TRANSMISSION: 2/26-4/2/1977

Consistently ranked among the very best *Doctor Who* stories of all time by fans and television historians, this superbly acted masterpiece of mystery and the macabre gives "Genesis of the Daleks" a run for its money as the high point of the Fourth Doctor's era. There are simply too many great moments and classic characters to discuss in detail here, though it's fair to say that the *Pygmalion*-inspired education of Leela and the villainous Mr. Sin (Deep Roy) rank near the top of the list of crowd-pleasing elements.

A. In what year was the Peking Homunculus created?

B. Guest star Deep Roy went on to appear as the diminutive Keenser in what 2009 big-screen reboot of a popular science-fiction franchise?

C. Magnus Greel's Time Cabinet is powered by what unstable type of energy?

D. The Doctor and Leela encounter what monstrous mammals in the London sewers?

E. John Bennett, who plays Li H'sen Chang here, previously appeared as a treacherous British General in what Third Doctor serial?

"The Horror of Fang Rock"

WRITER: Terrance Dicks
DIRECTOR: Paddy Russell
STARS: Tom Baker, Louise Jameson
ORIGINAL TRANSMISSION: 9/3-9/24/1977

In this extremely tense, atmospheric fright fest, the Doctor and Leela are among a group of travelers trapped inside a lighthouse with a shape-shifting alien monster. This is the kind of smart, suspenseful story that would work in any era of *Doctor Who*, but clever flourishes by writer Dicks and magnificent performances by Baker, Jameson, and guest star Colin Douglas prove it came at just the right time to become an all-time classic. Taut and terrific, this one is a must-see for horror aficionados.

A. What planet does the alien in the lighthouse come from?

B. Prior to appearing in this serial, guest star Annette Woollett acted in two episodes of what short-lived British horror anthology series, created by prolific film and television scribe Brian Clemens?

C. The Doctor quotes what Wilfrid Gibson poem in the final episode of this serial?

D. The Doctor uses what valuable objects to convert the lighthouse beam into a high-intensity laser?

E. What color are Leela's eyes at the end of this story?

"The Invisible Enemy"

WRITERS: Bob Baker, Dave Martin
DIRECTOR: Derrick Goodwin
STARS: Tom Baker, Louise Jameson, John Leeson
ORIGINAL TRANSMISSION: 10/1-10/22/1977

Enter the robot dog K-9 (voiced by Leeson) in this irresistibly goofy tale of a malignant, extraterrestrial germ infecting the crew of a base on Saturn's largest moon. It's a budget-minded variant of *Fantastic Voyage*, featuring loads of wonky pseudo-science, some inventive chroma key sequences, and an utterly ridiculous shrimp-like monster unlikely to frighten even the youngest of fans. Still, its historical significance and its refusal to take itself too seriously make it enjoyable viewing for the open-minded.

A. According to this serial, in what year were the first successful cloning experiments carried out?

B. What scientist created K-9?

C. Guest star Michael Sheard appeared in how many *Doctor Who* serials, including this one (in which he plays Lowe)?

D. How long can the miniaturized clones of the Doctor and Leela survive inside the real Doctor's infected body?

E. Kenneth Waller, who plays Hedges here, is best known for playing "Old" Mr. Grace on what long-running British sitcom?

"Image of the Fendahl"

WRITER: Chris Boucher
DIRECTOR: George Spenton-Foster
STARS: Tom Baker, Louise Jameson, John Leeson
ORIGINAL TRANSMISSION: 10/29-11/19/1977

A prehistoric skull possesses research scientists working in a priory outside of a small English village. This slick shocker is one of the better attempts at Hammer-style horror by the *Doctor Who* production team. Colorful supporting characters and huge, slithering monsters liven up an exceptionally well-acted gothic reworking of the classic Quatermass plot structure. Mature and moody, this is an oft-overlooked gem.

A. Guest star Wanda Ventham is the mother of what star of the 2010 BBC series *Sherlock*, created by frequent *Doctor Who* writer Mark Gatiss and executive producer Steven Moffat?

B. The Doctor and his friends use what ordinary household substance to kill the worm-like Fendahleen?

C. The skull being examined by Dr. Fendelman and his staff was found in what African country?

D. Geoffrey Hinsliff, who plays Jack Tyler, also appears in what later Fourth Doctor serial?

E. An x-ray of the skull reveals what unusual marking?

"The Sun Makers"

WRITER: Robert Holmes
DIRECTOR: Pennant Roberts
STARS: Tom Baker, Louise Jameson, John Leeson
ORIGINAL TRANSMISSION: 11/26-12/17/1977

The greedy, corporate overseers of a vast human settlement on Pluto use excessive taxes to oppress the population. Though this clever indictment of Britain's Inland Revenue department delivers little in the way of pulse-pounding action or stunning visuals, it's easily the best intentionally satirical outing in the original series. Writer Holmes somehow manages to make a dreadfully bleak, dystopian future hilarious, and the cast is uniformly excellent.

A. What is the reward offered for the capture of the Doctor?

B. By what method is Leela scheduled to be executed by the Company?

C. Guest star Richard Leech's many film credits include a role what 1957 supernatural horror classic, directed by Jacques Tourneur?

D. What accomplished actor and prestigious theater professor portrays the ruthless Collector, a vile alien fungus, in this serial?

E. To what planet did the Company first move Earth's surviving populace prior to relocating to Pluto?

"Underworld"

WRITERS: Bob Baker, Dave Martin
DIRECTOR: Norman Stewart
STARS: Tom Baker, Louise Jameson, John Leeson
ORIGINAL TRANSMISSION: 1/-1/28/1978

The Doctor, Leela, and K-9 help a Minyan starship crew complete an epic quest to recover the genetic race banks which hold the key to the survival of their race. Inspired by the legend of Jason and the Golden Fleece, this reasonably entertaining outing is noteworthy primarily for its unprecedented use of chroma key compositing to create most of its alien environs. Though hardly a classic, it does feature a couple of nice character moments for Jameson.

A. Jackson and his crew are searching for what lost ship?

B. Guest star Alan Lake was married to what busty British sex symbol, from 1968 until her death in 1984?

C. What is the rather redundant mantra of the R1C crew, repeated many times throughout this story?

D. Norman Stewart went on to direct Louise Jameson in two episodes of what short-lived British science-fiction series of the late 1970s?

E. The ancient Minyans expelled what alien race from Minyos more than 100,000 years before the events of this story?

"The Invasion of Time"

WRITER: David Agnew
DIRECTOR: Gerald Blake
ORIGINAL TRANSMISSION: 2/4-3/11/1978

In this fun but flawed epic, the Doctor cleverly prevents an attack on Gallifrey by the alien Vardans, only to discover that they were unwitting vanguard of a Sontaran invasion. Budget constraints prevent the production team from fully realizing a protracted chase within the bowels of the TARDIS, and the final fate of departing companion Leela smacks false. On the plus side, Baker and Jameson are both in top form, and much of the oft-bemoaned humor actually works quite well.

A. The Doctor was first elected president of Gallifrey in what earlier serial?

B. David Agnew is a pseudonym for what two writers?

C. What actress plays Rodan, the youthful Time Lady who travels with Leela to the wastelands outside the Citadel?

D. What forbidden weapon does the Doctor instruct K-9 and Rodan to construct?

E. What does the Doctor find waiting for him in a crate, inside the TARDIS, at the end of this story?

"The Ribos Operation"

WRITER: Robert Holmes
DIRECTOR: George Spenton-Foster
STARS: Tom Baker, Mary Tamm, John Leeson
ORIGINAL TRANSMISSION: 9/2-9/23/1978

The season-long quest for the Key to Time begins with this clever crime caper involving interstellar con men angling to sell useless mineral rights to an exiled politician. The stunning Tamm brings a healthy dose of Emma Peel-style glamour to the role of new companion Romana, but Iain Cuthbertson steals the show as the slick and supremely charismatic Garron. The crocodilian shrivenzale which guards the chamber containing the crown jewels is silly but surprisingly endearing.

A. What is the full name of the Doctor's new companion?

B. How old does Romana say the Doctor is, prompting him to counter with the assertion that he's only 756?

C. Garron claims Ribos is rich with what precious mineral element?

D. Guest star Iain Cuthbertson was a regular on what 1980s children's show about an elderly woman with superhuman powers?

E. Guest star John Hamill appeared with two-time *Doctor Who* villain Michael Gough in what 1970 cult film about a prehistoric man running amok in contemporary England?

"The Pirate Planet"

WRITER: Douglas Adams
DIRECTOR: Pennant Roberts
STARS: Tom Baker, Mary Tamm, John Leeson
ORIGINAL TRANSMISSION: 9/30-10/21/1978

You don't need to read the credits to realize this off-kilter tale of planet-snatching is the work of the late Douglas Adams. As the Doctor, Romana, and K-9 continue their search for the segments of the Key to Time, they run afoul of a demented, disfigured space pirate on the planet Calufrax. The bellicose Bruce Purchase and a murderous mechanical parrot are among the highlights of this funny, fast-paced adventure.

A. Romana claims the Doctor has been operating the TARDIS for how long?

B. The Captain (Bruce Purchase) suffered the injuries resulting in his current state when his ship crash landed on what planet?

C. Rosalind Lloyd, who plays the Captain's nurse, went on to appear in what salacious 1981 science-fiction film about a woman impregnated by an alien monster on a remote planet?

D. Guest star David Warwick later appears as a police commissioner in what Tenth Doctor story?

E. The Doctor claims to have helped what Earth scientist make his most celebrated discovery by dropping an apple on his head?

"The Stones of Blood"

WRITER: David Fisher
DIRECTOR: Darrol Blake
STARS: Tom Baker, Mary Tamm, John Leeson
ORIGINAL TRANSMISSION: 10/28-11/18/1978

This third installment of the Key to Time arc begins as a typically atmospheric horror tale, but becomes a spirited courtroom drama in the final episode. Baker spends a fair amount of the story acting opposite disembodied voices, an unusual format that perfectly suits an actor accustomed to being the center of attention. Beatrix Lehmann and Susan Engel are quite good in guest-starring roles.

A. In addition to murder, Cessair of Diplos (Susan Engel) was convicted for stealing what sacred object?

B. David Fisher went on to script which episode of the television series *Hammer House of Horror*, starring two-time *Doctor Who* guest star Paul Darrow?

C. The Ogri are living stone beings from what distant star system?

D. The Doctor claims to have met what seventeenth-century historian and author, who first postulated that Stonehenge and other, similar monuments were built by druids?

E. Guest star Gerald Cross previously appeared in "Roman Wall," a 1956 episode of what historical adventure series starring longtime *Doctor Who* companion actor William Russell?

"The Androids of Tara"

WRITER: David Fisher
DIRECTOR: Michael Hayes
STARS: Tom Baker, Mary Tamm, John Leeson
ORIGINAL TRANSMISSION: 11/25-12/16/1978

The highlight of the entire Key to Time season, this campy twist on *The Prisoner of Zenda* sends the Doctor and Romana to a feudal world where a conniving Count conspires to use robot doubles of a prince and his beloved to ascend to the throne. Peter Jeffrey is simply marvelous as the despicable, duplicitous Grendel, while Tamm gets her turn in the spotlight in a dual role as Time Lady and princess-to-be.

A. The fourth segment of the Key to Time is disguised as what object?

B. Peter Jeffrey previously appeared in what lost Second Doctor serial?

C. The Doctor attempts to enjoy what recreational activity while Romana searches for the Key?

D. The Doctor hits the android Romana on the head with what royal object?

E. In 1961, Michael Hayes directed all seven episodes of what BBC science-fiction serial, starring Julie Christie and frequent *Doctor Who* guest star Peter Halliday?

"The Power of Kroll"

WRITER: Robert Holmes
DIRECTOR: Norman Stewart
STARS: Tom Baker, Mary Tamm, John Leeson
ORIGINAL TRANSMISSION: 12/23/1978-1/13/1979

On a swampy moon, the Doctor and Romana search for the fifth segment of the Key to Time and battle a marauding, mammoth octopus. Outstanding special effects take center stage here, with the towering, tentacled Kroll likely to leave quite an impression on viewers accustomed to monsters on a much more modest scale. K-9 remains in the TARDIS this time out, giving Leeson a chance to appear on-screen as the ill-fated refinery worker Dugeen.

A. What frequent *Doctor Who* guest star, best known for playing ruthless villains, portrays Fenner in this serial?

B. Human visitors to Delta 3 refer to the green-skinned natives by what rather derogatory name?

C. Script editor Anthony Read went on to write three 1980s television serials based on what John Wyndham science-fiction novel?

D. What is the Doctor's lucky number?

E. The mercenary Rohm-Dutt (Glyn Owen) is selling what to the natives of Delta Three?

"The Armageddon Factor"

WRITERS: Bob Baker, Dave Martin
DIRECTOR: Michael Hayes
STARS: Tom Baker, Mary Tamm, John Leeson
ORIGINAL TRANSMISSION: 1/20-2/24/1979

The final segment of the Key to Time is somewhere on the planet Atrios, a war-ravaged world locked in a perpetual stalemate with the neighboring world of Zeos. Longer and more ambitious than the season's previous tales, this one is unfortunately not as much fun. John Woodvine is fine as the increasingly mad commander of Atrios' depleted military, and Lalla Ward effectively auditions to replace the departing Tamm, but it all ends a bit abruptly to satisfactorily conclude such a sweeping story arc.

A. Drax (Barry Jackson) refers to the Doctor by what nickname?

B. Guest star William Squire provided the voice of what wizened character in Ralph Bakshi's animated film adaptation of *The Lord of the Rings* (1978)?

C. Valentine Dyall, who portrays the Black Guardian, appears with Claire Bloom ("The End of Time") in what classic 1963 horror film, based on a Shirley Jackson novel?

D. The Doctor constructs a temporary substitute for the final segment of the Key from what substance?

E. What are the interstellar coordinates for the planet Zeos?

"Destiny of the Daleks"

WRITER: Terry Nation
DIRECTOR: Ken Grieve
STARS: Tom Baker, Lalla Ward
ORIGINAL TRANSMISSION: 9/1-9/22/1979

The Doctor and Romana land on Skaro, where the Daleks have revived their creator to gain his assistance in defeating a powerful new enemy. The influence of new script editor Douglas Adams can be felt throughout, with bits of high camp thrown in at nearly every turn. The Movellans look rather kitschy today, and the basic plot about a computer-driven stalemate on the battlefield was used in the previous season's final story, but the energetic performances of Baker and Ward (as the newly regenerated Romana) make this one a worthwhile diversion.

A. What book does the Doctor read while trapped under a fallen column in the ruins on Skaro?

B. According to the Doctor, what planet won the Galactic Olympic Games?

C. What device has the Doctor installed in the TARDIS to elude the Black Guardian?

D. Guest star Tony Osoba later appears in what Seventh Doctor serial?

E. Terry Nation moved to the United States in 1980, where he produced six episodes of what iconic action television series?

"City of Death"

WRITER: David Agnew
DIRECTOR: Michael Hayes
STARS: Tom Baker, Lalla Ward
ORIGINAL TRANSMISSION: 9/29-10/20/1979

Oddly, many critics and fans panned this stellar outing when it first aired, despite the fact that its final episode garnered the highest ratings in the series' history, and it has gone on to become one of the most popular serials ever. The Doctor, Romana, and a police inspector prevent the last survivor of a ruthless alien race from irreparably altering Earth's history to save his people. Sharp humor, crisp pacing, and magnificent guest turns from Julian Glover, Tom Chadbon, and Catherine Schell add up to a cracking good time.

A. Romana tells Duggan (Tom Chadbon) she's how old?

B. Which *Monty Python's Flying Circus* cast member makes a cameo appearance in this serial?

c. The Doctor claims to have helped William Shakespeare write what famous tragedy?

d. Julian Glover's son, Jamie, played Phillipe Gervais in seventeen episodes of what 1990s science-fiction soap opera?

e. What does the Doctor write on the blank canvases in Leonardo Da Vinci's workshop?

"The Creature from the Pit"

writer: David Fisher
director: Christopher Barry
stars: Tom Baker, Lalla Ward, David Brierly
original transmission: 10/27-11/17/1979

The Doctor, Romana, and K-9 (Brierly) attempt to free an imprisoned alien monster from the control of a tyrannical noblewoman on a jungle planet. Giant blobs, murderous rolling weeds, scavenging simpletons, and very theatrical performances from Baker, Ward, and guest villainess Myra Frances make this engaging mystery memorable. Guest star Geoffrey Bayldon unintentionally evokes memories of former Doctor William Hartnell in a sympathetic supporting role.

a. Erato comes from what planet?

b. This was the final *Doctor Who* serial for what actor and stunt coordinator, who worked on a total of twenty-six episodes between 1966 and 1979?

c. What three-time *Doctor Who* director appears in an onscreen role in this serial, playing an engineer?

d. What material is valued above all others on Chloris?

e. What does the Doctor say is his lucky number, contradicting a similar statement from an earlier adventure?

"Nightmare of Eden"

WRITER: Bob Baker
DIRECTORS: Alan Bromly, Graham Williams
STARS: Tom Baker, Lalla Ward, David Brierly
ORIGINAL TRANSMISSION: 11/27-12/15/1979

The Doctor and his companions battle galactic drug smugglers and rampaging monsters as they attempt to separate two spaceships which have collided in hyperspace. Though perhaps not quite a "very special episode" of *Doctor Who*, this well-acted anti-drug outing functions equally well as a cautionary tale and popcorn entertainment piece. The shaggy Mandrels are admittedly rather silly, though the case can be made that this adds to their charm.

A. How many passengers is the *Empress* carrying?

B. Alan Bromly produced the 1967 pilot *Girl in a Black Bikini*, which starred which former *Doctor Who* companion actor?

C. What deadly drug is being smuggled aboard the *Empress*?

D. The Doctor claims to work for what cosmic company?

E. David Daker, who plays Captain Rigg here, appeared in the Third Doctor serial "The Time Warrior" as what medieval criminal?

"The Horns of Nimon"

WRITER: Anthony Read
DIRECTOR: Kenny McBain
STARS: Tom Baker, Lalla Ward, David Brierly
ORIGINAL TRANSMISSION: 12/22/1979-1/12/1980

Goofy-looking monsters and Greek mythology are once again the order of the day in this semi-comedic tale of a horned alien posing as an all-powerful god to facilitate the invasion of a vulnerable world. Graham Crowden and Malcolm Terris swallow great mouthfuls of scenery and routinely upstage their co-stars as a power-hungry priest and a brutish freighter pilot, respectively. This amenable but average serial became the default season-ender when a strike shut down production before Douglas Adams' "Shada" could be completed.

A. What planet did the Nimon conquer before coming to Skonnos?

B. The Doctor laments that he forgot to remind the ancient Greek hero Theseus to do what?

C. Guest star Janet Ellis, who plays the smitten Teka, went on to co-host what long-running children's series from 1983 to 2001?

D. Sezom (John Bailey) gives Romana a piece of what mineral element so that she can increase the power of Soldeed's staff and temporarily incapacitate the Nimon?

E. Which guest star in this serial was originally offered the role of the Doctor when Jon Pertwee departed in 1974, but turned it down because he didn't want to make a three-year commitment to the series?

"The Leisure Hive"

WRITER: David Fisher
DIRECTOR: Lovett Bickford
STARS: Tom Baker, Lalla Ward, John Leeson
ORIGINAL TRANSMISSION: 8/30-9/20/1980

The Doctor and Romana investigate mysterious deaths and dangerous tachyon experiments at a holiday retreat on the planet Argolis. New producer John Nathan-Turner overhauls the series for the Fourth Doctor's final season with synthesized music, state-of-the-art (for BBC television in 1980) visual effects, and a cerebral plot satirizing the Mafia and the decline of British tourism. The make-up used to prematurely age Baker's Doctor is excellent, and the overall quality of the serial is a marked improvement over the previous season's final stories. Leeson's return to the role of K-9 is an added plus.

A. How long did the war between the Argolins and the Foamasi last?

B. The primary tourist attraction on Argolis is what sophisticated machine, capable of rejuvenating organic matter?

C. What symbols, present throughout the remainder of the original series in various forms, were first added to the Doctor's costume in this serial?

D. Guest star Adrienne Corri appeared in what 1954 British cult film about an alien *femme fatale* menacing guests at a remote country inn?

E. Corri and three-time guest star Laurence Payne co-starred with what regular *Doctor Who* cast member in the 1972 Hammer film *The Vampire Circus*?

"Meglos"

WRITERS: John Flanagan, Andrew McCulloch
DIRECTOR: Terence Dudley
STARS: Tom Baker, Lalla Ward, John Leeson
ORIGINAL TRANSMISSION: 9/27-10/18/1980

Former companion actress Jacqueline Hill returns to the series as the zealous leader of a group of religious fanatics in this tale of a ruthless alien attempting to steal a sacred crystal from the citizens of the planet Tigella. Best remembered as the story in which Baker is temporarily transformed into a walking cactus, this modestly diverting adventure treads on very familiar ground, but features enough solid performances to be worth a look.

A. Meglos hails from what desert planet?

B. The Deons believe what benevolent god has provided them with the crystalline Dodecahedron?

C. Jacqueline Hill remains the only *Doctor Who* regular to return to the series in a different role, but which two Tenth Doctor guest players went on to play full-time companions?

D. The Doctor and Romana receive a message instructing them to return to what planet in the closing moments of this story?

E. Guest star Crawford Logan is a member of what alien-sounding Scottish rock band?

"Full Circle"

WRITER: Andrew Smith
DIRECTOR: Peter Grimwade
STARS: Tom Baker, Lalla Ward, John Leeson, Matthew Waterhouse
ORIGINAL TRANSMISSION: 10/25-11/15/1980

The first installment of the E-Space trilogy has the Doctor, Romana, and K-9 battling huge spiders, reptilian Marshmen, and bureaucratic deceit on the swampy world of Alzarius. Waterhouse doesn't quite find his rhythm here as new companion Adric, but Ward and Baker are typically excellent, and the Marshmen's relentless assault on the grounded Starliner is quite exciting.

A. Guest star Leonard Maguire also appears in what 1980 horror film which is based on a Bram Stoker novel, but shares its title with a 1983 Fifth Doctor serial?

B. Adric wears what gold award on his shirt, to demonstrate his exceptional computational skills?

C. The TARDIS enters E-Space by passing through what rare cosmic anomaly?

D. The crashed Starliner is originally from what planet?

E. George Baker, who plays Login here, previously starred in what 1965 science-fiction sequel about humanoid monsters created by failed teleportation experiments?

"State of Decay"

WRITER: Terrance Dicks
DIRECTOR: Peter Moffatt
STARS: Tom Baker, Lalla Ward, Matthew Waterhouse, John Leeson
ORIGINAL TRANSMISSION: 11/22-12/13/1980

Villagers from a feudal society on an Earth-like planet are periodically selected to be taken to an ominous tower, where they become food for the blood-thirsty Lord Aukon and his pale, corpse-like cohorts. The best installment of the three-part E-Space arc revels gleefully in its gothic horror trappings, providing a host of Hammer-inspired chills while simultaneously giving traditional vampire mythos a *Planet of the Apes*-style makeover. Waterhouse is excellent here, playing Adric as a calculating, potentially duplicitous mischief maker.

A. What beings destroyed the Great Vampires of old in a legendary war?

B. According to K-9, legends of vampires persist on how many inhabited planets?

C. Guest star Clinton Greyn appeared in the Sixth Doctor serial "The Two Doctors" as what type of alien creature?

D. The Tower is actually what lost Earth space vessel?

E. Arthur Hewlett, who plays Kalmar here, later appears in which Sixth Doctor serial?

"Warriors' Gate"

WRITER: Stephen Gallagher
DIRECTORS: Paul Joyce, Graeme Harper
STARS: Tom Baker, Lalla Ward, Matthew Waterhouse, John Leeson
ORIGINAL TRANSMISSION: 1/3-1/24/1981

Things get a bit too existential in this slow-paced but visually striking final chapter of the E-Space trilogy. The Doctor and his companions help a race of time sensitive slaves escape from ruthless slave traders trapped at the gateway between our universe and the rapidly collapsing E-Space dimension. Ward delivers a fine final performance as the departing Romana, but the story's lofty aspirations undermine its entertainment value.

A. The Doctor pays Romana what compliment as he prepared to leave her and K-9 in E-Space?

B. Guest star Kenneth Cope appeared in what 1956 Hammer science-fiction film, alongside a very young Frazer Hines?

C. Lalla Ward married what actor a short time before this serial first aired?

D. Prior to the collapse of their empire, the Tharils regularly raided N-Space to procure what commodity?

E. The robotic knights who guard the Gateway are called what?

"The Keeper of Traken"

WRITER: Johnny Byrne
DIRECTOR: John Black
STARS: Tom Baker, Matthew Waterhouse, Sarah Sutton
ORIGINAL TRANSMISSION: 1/31-2/21/1981

An old enemy of the Doctor returns to disrupt the peaceful transfer of power on a tranquil alien world. The signs of Baker's imminent departure are beginning to show here, with the ordinarily boisterous Fourth Doctor appearing far more brooding and contemplative throughout. Anthony Ainley's debut as the revived Master is a rousing success, and Waterhouse does some of his best work in his only story as the Time Lord's primary traveling companion.

A. The Melkur is really what alien object?

B. Guest star Dennis Carey later appears in what Sixth Doctor serial, set on the planet Karfel?

C. Nyssa (Sarah Sutton) is the daughter of what citizen of Traken?

D. The Traken Union is located in what star system?

E. Margot Van der Burgh, who plays Katura here, appeared in the First Doctor serial "The Aztecs" as what character?

"Logopolis"

WRITER: Christopher H. Bidmead
DIRECTOR: Peter Grimwade
STARS: Tom Baker, Matthew Waterhouse, Sarah Sutton, Janet Fielding
ORIGINAL TRANSMISSION: 2/28-3/21/1981

The Master attempts to use the reality-bending power of a race of cosmic mathematicians to hold the universe hostage. A cerebral and suspenseful send off for the longest-tenured Time Lord of all, this apocalyptic adventure is the best of Baker's final year. Fielding's entrance as an unwilling stowaway on the TARDIS brings a bit of levity to a rather grim and gritty story. Decades later, the Fourth Doctor's "death" retains its gasp-inducing shock value.

A. In what Third Doctor serial does the Doctor first materialize his TARDIS around the Master's?

B. Tegan, mistaking the TARDIS for a real police box, enters the ship seeking assistance with what problem?

C. The mysterious Watcher is played by what actor, who also appears in "Full Circle" as Rysik?

D. With the block-transfer calculations on Logopolis halted, the entire universe is threatened by an excess of what thermodynamic property?

E. Prior to joining the cast of *Doctor Who* as Tegan Jovanka, Janet Fielding played a secretary in what episode of the anthology series *Hammer House of Horror*?

(Answers begin on Page 228.)

The Fifth Doctor

1981-1984, 2007

PRODUCER JOHN NATHAN-TURNER WANTED TO REPLACE the larger-than-life Tom Baker with an actor who could bring vulnerability and humanity to the role of the Doctor. He chose youthful, fresh-faced actor Peter Davison, best known to audiences on both sides of the Atlantic for his role in the TV adaptation of James Herriot's *All Creatures Great and Small.* Davison ably fit the bill, creating a Time Lord who always rose to a challenge, but seldom seemed three steps ahead of his enemies the way his predecessor had in his later years. Because he appeared so young, the Fifth Doctor's companions were more apt to question his judgment, creating a dysfunctional family dynamic in the TARDIS which often served to make combating external threats even more difficult.

After exiting *Doctor Who*, Davison returned to *All Creatures Great and Small*, and has followed that up with starring roles in other popular series such as *At Home with the Braithwaites* and *The Last Detective*. Davison returned to the TARDIS briefly as the Fifth Doctor in the 2007 holiday short, "Time Crash."

The Fifth Doctor succumbed to spectrox toxemia while saving his companion, Peri, on the planet Androzani Minor.

"Castrovalva"

WRITER: Christopher H. Bidmead
DIRECTOR: Fiona Cumming
STARS: Peter Davison, Janet Fielding, Matthew Waterhouse, Sarah Sutton
ORIGINAL TRANSMISSION: 1/4-1/12/1982

The Doctor and his companions visit a tranquil planet to stabilize his latest regeneration, but walk right into a trap laid by an old enemy. Davison does some fine work in this cerebral, M.C. Escher-inspired outing, channeling several of the Doctor's past selves and even literally unraveling his immediate predecessor's trademark scarf. Though hardly high adventure, this ambitious effort is a highlight of the Fifth Doctor's solid first season.

A. How much of the TARDIS's mass is jettisoned to escape total destruction at Event One?

B. The Doctor adds what unusual adornment to his lapel in this serial?

C. Unstable from his regeneration, the Doctor mistakenly refers to Tegan as which two former companions?

D. Guest star Dallas Cavell previously appeared as Sir James Quinlan in what Third Doctor serial?

E. Guest star Souska John is the niece of what former *Doctor Who* companion actress?

"Four to Doomsday"

WRITER: Terence Dudley
DIRECTOR: John Black
STARS: Peter Davison, Janet Fielding, Matthew Waterhouse, Sarah Sutton
ORIGINAL TRANSMISSION: 1/18-1/26/1982

It's a pity this intellectual offering is overlooked by many fans, because it features some excellent interplay between Davison and Waterhouse, and guest star Stratford Johns chews the scenery as a bellicose, frog-like alien with a God complex. Like the story that preceded it, this measured tale is more thought-provoking than pulse-pounding, but there are enough fantastic elements and moments of genuine suspense to keep younger viewers interested.

A. The Doctor claims to be near-sighted in which eye?

B. Guest star Annie Lambert's character shares her name with what 1983 Fifth Doctor serial?

C. What was the number of the Air Australia flight Tegan was on her way to catch when she inadvertently stowed away in the TARDIS?

D. Burt Kwouk, who plays Lin Futu here, is best known for what recurring role in Blake Edwards' *Pink Panther* films?

E. What classic text by English mathematician Alfred North Whitehead is among the books aboard the TARDIS?

"Kinda"

WRITER: Christopher Bailey
DIRECTOR: Peter Grimwade
STARS: Peter Davison, Janet Fielding, Matthew Waterhouse, Sarah Sutton
ORIGINAL TRANSMISSION: 2/1-2/9/1982

Fielding is excellent in this tale of demonic possession on a jungle planet where Earth colonists and angry natives brace for war. With his companions off dealing with their own problems, the Doctor gets a temporary assistant in the form of Welsh actress Nerys Hughes, and the dynamic between Time Lord and slightly more mature sidekick is a refreshing change. Winning guest turns by Simon Rouse and Richard Todd throughout help make up for a rather unconvincing giant snake in the story's closing moments.

A. Nerys Hughes later appears in what 2008 episode of *Torchwood*?

B. What is the name of the malevolent entity that possesses Tegan on Deva Loka?

C. Richard Todd, whose character goes quite mad in this serial, played a philandering husband in the first segment of what 1972 Amicus horror anthology film?

D. As a child, Tegan didn't like what sweet dessert food?

E. What succinct name do the Kinda use to describe outsiders to their world?

"The Visitation"

WRITER: Eric Saward
DIRECTOR: Peter Moffatt
STARS: Peter Davison, Janet Fielding, Matthew Waterhouse, Sarah Sutton
ORIGINAL TRANSMISSION: 2/16-2/23/1982

The Doctor, his companions, and a roguish highwayman battle alien reptiles in seventeenth-century England. Widely regarded as one of the best Fifth Doctor serials, this thrilling throwback showcases excellent performances and memorable villains. An intriguing thread about the paradox between the Terileptils' love of art and their penchant for violent conquest goes largely unexplored, but with all the fast-paced action going on, you won't really care.

A. Who plays the actor-turned-bandit Richard Mace?

B. What device makes its final appearance of the original series in this story?

C. The Grim Reaper-like specter that attacks Squire John (John Savident) and his family is actually what?

D. The Doctor and his companions inadvertently cause what real-life disaster in this serial?

E. Which 1980s *Doctor Who* actor originally adopted his stage name in order to avoid confusion with "The Visitation" director Peter Moffatt, who also dabbled in acting early in his career?

"Black Orchid"

WRITER: Terence Dudley
DIRECTOR: Ron Jones
STARS: Peter Davison, Janet Fielding, Matthew Waterhouse, Sarah Sutton
ORIGINAL TRANSMISSION: 3/1-3/2/1982

In the first (and, to date, only) historical tale since the 1960s not to feature any science-fiction elements, the Doctor and his companions stumble onto a series of bizarre murders in an early twentieth-century manor house. Admittedly a minor entry, much of the fun here is derived from watching Davison play cricket, Fielding dance the Charleston, Waterhouse gorge himself at a buffet table, and Sutton quite literally have a conversation with herself.

A. Nyssa is an exact double of what young woman the Doctor and his companions meet in 1925?

B. George Cranleigh (Gareth Milne) found the Black Orchid while exploring what South American river?

C. Guest star Michael Cochrane later appears in what Seventh Doctor serial set in an English manor house?

D. What alcoholic cocktail does Tegan order at Lord Cranleigh's party?

E. Guest star Moray Watson went on to appear in what 1982 episode of the anthology series *Tales of the Unexpected*, alongside frequent *Doctor Who* guest performer Alan Rowe?

"Earthshock"

WRITER: Eric Saward
DIRECTOR: Peter Grimwade
STARS: Peter Davison, Janet Fielding, Matthew Waterhouse, Sarah Sutton
ORIGINAL TRANSMISSION: 3/8-3/16/1982

This nearly perfect tale pits the Doctor and his companions against a battalion of newly designed Cybermen aboard a space freighter hurtling toward Earth. Though Waterhouse's Adric is almost insufferable in the opening scenes, his final moments will move even the most jaded viewer to tears. Guest star Beryl Reid does a bang-up job as the tough-as-nails starship captain, while Davison and David Banks' wonderfully ruthless Cyber Leader enjoy an unforgettable verbal tête-à-tête.

A. What are Adric's final words in this serial?

B. What regular element of the series' title sequences was deliberately omitted from the closing credits of this story's final episode, in tribute to the ill-fated Adric?

C. Guest star James Warwick previously starred in what 1981 Robert Holmes-written, Douglas Camfield-directed TV movie, which shares its title with a 2010 *The Sarah Jane Adventures* outing?

D. Clare Clifford, who plays Professor Kyle here, later appears in what 2008 episode of *Torchwood*?

E. What gold-plated object does the Doctor use to temporarily incapacitate the Cyber Leader?

"Time-Flight"

WRITER: Peter Grimwade
DIRECTOR: Ron Jones
STARS: Peter Davison, Janet Fielding, Sarah Sutton
ORIGINAL TRANSMISSION: 3/22-3/30/1982

While investigating the disappearance of the Concorde, the Doctor and his companions are transported to prehistoric Earth and menaced by an evil wizard. Considered by fans and Davison himself to be a misfire, this admittedly goofy adventure is really quite enjoyable if taken in the right spirit. From the appearance of the TARDIS in the Heathrow Airport terminal to the over-the-top histrionics of the villainous Kalid, it's popcorn fluff that suffers primarily from being sandwiched between two of the strongest outings of the Fifth Doctor's tenure.

A. What actor (credited under the pseudonym "Leon Ny Taiy" in the first episode) plays the wizard Kalid?

B. How do Tegan and Nyssa know that the seemingly reincarnated Adric is an illusion?

C. Guest star Nigel Stock appeared in what 1968 Hammer science-fiction film, alongside recurring *Doctor Who* villain Anthony Ainley?

D. The Doctor and his companions are enlisted by what division of U.N.I.T. to investigate the missing Concorde?

E. Which companion does the Doctor leave behind at the end of this serial?

"Arc of Infinity"

WRITER: Johnny Byrne
DIRECTOR: Ron Jones
STARS: Peter Davison, Janet Fielding, Sarah Sutton
ORIGINAL TRANSMISSION: 1/3-1/12/1983

The Doctor battles corruption on his home planet and the renegade Time Lord Omega in the Netherlands. Ian Collier, Michael Gough, and future Doctor Colin Baker all deliver memorable guest turns in this taut tale of intrigue and action that expertly exploits both the rich mythology established in the Gallifrey stories of the 1970s and the scenic Amsterdam locations. Any time the lead actor plays both the Doctor and the villain, you know you're in for a good time.

A. Who is the new Lord High President of Gallifrey?

B. What *Doctor Who* producer makes an Alfred Hitchcock-like cameo appearance in this serial?

C. The Doctor inquires about which former companion, who he left on Gallifrey at the end of his last visit?

D. Guest star Paul Jerricho reprises his roles as the Castellan in what later Fifth Doctor adventure?

E. Max Harvey, who plays Cardinal Zorac in this serial, appears in what 2004 made-for-television mystery movie, alongside frequent *Doctor Who* guest star Michael Wisher's son, Andrew?

"Snakedance"

WRITER: Christopher Bailey
DIRECTOR: Fiona Cumming
STARS: Peter Davison, Janet Fielding, Sarah Sutton
ORIGINAL TRANSMISSION: 1/18-1/26/1983

The serpentine Mara returns to once again torment Tegan on the eve of a historic celebration on the planet Manussa. Fielding again shines when given center stage, while Martin Clunes' bravura turn as the acerbic, effeminate aristocrat Lon is one of the more memorable guest appearances of the 1980s. The snake prop is appreciably better this time than in the Mara's previous outing, but the overall production suffers a bit from a rather abrupt ending.

A. The planet Manussa is in what star system?

B. Guest star Martin Clunes went on to star in what popular British sitcom, created by "Amy's Choice" writer Simon Nye?

C. Brian Miller, who portrays Dugdale here, is married to what longtime companion actress?

D. How long ago did the Manussans defeat the Mara and banish it from their world?

E. The Tenth Doctor mentions the Mara while talking to himself in what 2007 adventure?

"Mawdryn Undead"

WRITER: Peter Grimwade
DIRECTOR: Peter Moffatt
STARS: Peter Davison, Janet Fielding, Sarah Sutton, Nicholas Courtney, Mark Strickson
ORIGINAL TRANSMISSION: 2/1-2/9/1983

The Doctor gets a new companion, reunites with an old friend, and begins a three-story rematch with a vengeful enemy in this effective tale of time travel and the price of eternal life. The Black Guardian recruits a rebellious schoolboy to murder the Time Lord, who has his hands full with an alien scientist bent on stealing his remaining regenerations. Courtney's first appearance in *Doctor Who* since "Terror of the Zygons" is a treat.

A. Guest star David Collings previously appeared in the Fourth Doctor serial "Revenge of the Cybermen" as what antagonistic character?

B. Brigadier Lethbridge-Stewart has retired from military service to teach what subject at Brendon Public School?

C. Turlough (Mark Strickson) attempts to murder the Doctor with what everyday object as the Time Lord tries to repair the transmat device?

D. Guest star Sheila Gill appears in what episode of the short-lived 1990s science-fiction series *Crime Traveller*?

E. The Brigadier states that Benton left U.N.I.T. in what year?

"Terminus"

WRITER: Stephen Gallagher
DIRECTOR: Mary Ridge
STARS: Peter Davison, Janet Fielding, Sarah Sutton, Mark Strickson
ORIGINAL TRANSMISSION: 2/15-2/23/1983

The Doctor and his companions land on a seemingly deserted space station, only to discover that it's become an intergalactic leper colony. Grim and oppressive, this downbeat offering benefits considerably from the fine work of the departing Sutton. Fielding and Strickson spend much of the runtime stuck in a tiny crawlspace beneath the station's decks, adding to the claustrophobic atmosphere but contributing little to the narrative.

A. Terminus, Inc. claims to be able to cure what debilitating ailment?

B. Guest star Liza Goddard was once married to what *Doctor Who* star?

C. Turlough is given which former companion's old room aboard the TARDIS?

D. The Vanir are kept alive with what drug?

E. How many episodes of the Terry Nation-created science-fiction series *Blake's 7* did "Terminus" director Mary Ridge helm?

"Enlightenment"

WRITER: Barbara Clegg
DIRECTOR: Fiona Cumming
STARS: Peter Davison, Janet Fielding, Mark Strickson
ORIGINAL TRANSMISSION: 3/1-3/9/1983

Davison's sophomore season reaches its creative peak with this rousing, off-beat tale of an interstellar boat race for intellectual and spiritual enlightenment. Topnotch production design and first-rate visual effects are on display throughout, but it's the fine performances of all three leads and guest star Lynda Baron that make this one so much fun to watch. The final resolution of Turlough's conflict with the Black Guardian is intelligent and immensely satisfying.

A. What do the Eternals call mortal beings?

B. What is the name of Captain Wrack's ship?

C. Guest star Keith Barron played a ship's purser in what 1976 Oscar-nominated drama, which shares its title with a far less serious-minded Tenth Doctor story?

D. Guest star Tony Caunter's first *Doctor Who* role came in what First Doctor historical adventure?

E. The Doctor replaces what part of his apparel during the race?

"The King's Demons"

WRITER: Terence Dudley
DIRECTOR: Tony Virgo
STARS: Peter Davison, Janet Fielding, Mark Strickson, Gerald Flood
ORIGINAL TRANSMISSION: 3/15-3/16/1983

In the first act of a campaign to destabilize civilizations across the galaxy, the Master uses a robotic doppelganger of King John to prevent the signing of the Magna Carta. To argue that this threadbare bit of period silliness is anything other than a budget-minded excuse to re-use existing sets would be pointless, but Davison and Anthony Ainley at least have fun verbally jousting with one another. The notion of a shape-shifting android companion, though largely unrealized, remains an intriguing one.

A. What is the name of the shape-shifting robot in the employ of the Master?

B. The Master's TARDIS is disguised as what medieval torture device?

C. Guest star Frank Windsor previously appeared in the pilot episode of what supernatural detective series, created by former *Doctor Who* script editor Dennis Spooner?

D. Where is the real King John while his throne is occupied by a robotic impostor?

E. Guest star Gerald Flood played what character in the short-lived 1960s science-fiction series *City Beneath the Sea* and its sequel, *Secret Beneath the Sea*?

"The Five Doctors"

WRITER: Terrance Dicks
DIRECTOR: Peter Moffatt
STARS: Peter Davison, Tom Baker *(stock footage)*, Jon Pertwee, Patrick Troughton, William Hartnell *(stock footage)*, Richard Hurndall, Janet Fielding, Mark Strickson, Lalla Ward *(stock footage)*, Elisabeth Sladen, Carole Ann Ford, Nicholas Courtney, John Leeson
ORIGINAL TRANSMISSION: 11/23/1985

The Doctor's past incarnations and companions are scooped out of time and dropped in the Death Zone on Gallifrey, where they must work together to defeat their deadliest enemies and discover who's behind it all. This all-star romp somehow overcomes its excesses and delivers an entertaining, exceptionally well-crafted story. Though the absence of unavailable (Katy Manning, Deborah Watling) and unwilling (Baker, John Levene) veteran players and the necessary re-casting of the deceased

Hartnell's First Doctor keep it from fully realizing its fan-pleasing potential, Hurndall and the inventive production team do an admirable job of filling the gaps.

A. Dinah Sheridan, who plays Chancellor Flavia in this story, previously appeared alongside three-time *Doctor Who* guest star Kevin Stoney in what episode of *Hammer House of Horror*?

B. What objects, purported to contain forbidden Time Lord secrets, are found in the Castellan's chambers?

C. The Cybermen in the Death Zone are defeated by what ruthless alien machine?

D. The Fourth Doctor and Romana are caught in what temporal anomaly when someone attempts to scoop them from their time stream?

E. Guest star Richard Matthews previously appeared in what 1973 Hammer horror film, scripted by two-time *Doctor Who* scribe Don Houghton?

"Warriors of the Deep"

WRITER: Johnny Byrne
DIRECTOR: Pennant Roberts
STARS: Peter Davison, Janet Fielding, Mark Strickson
ORIGINAL TRANSMISSION: 1/5-1/13/1984

The Doctor and his companions face the combined might of the Silurians and the Sea Devils in an underwater military installation during a twenty-first-century cold war. If not for the rushed production schedule and unnecessarily bleak ending, this ambitious, oft-criticized tale might have been one of the best of the 1980s. As is, it's still better than advertised, with plenty of action and solid performances across the board.

A. In what year do the Doctor and his companions land in Sea Base 4?

B. The Silurians unleash what mammoth prehistoric marine beast on the crew of Sea Base 4?

C. Ingrid Pitt, who appears here as Doctor Solow, co-stars with Jon Pertwee and "The Creature from the Pit" guest player Geoffrey Bayldon in the fourth and final segment of what 1971 Amicus horror anthology film?

D. Guest star Nitza Saul went on to appear in "A Double Life," the seventh episode of what short-lived science-fiction police drama created by three-time *Doctor Who* scripter Chris Boucher?

E. The TARDIS is attacked by what robotic defense system when it materializes in space near the Earth?

"The Awakening"

WRITER: Eric Pringle
DIRECTOR: Michael Owen Morris
STARS: Peter Davison, Janet Fielding, Mark Strickson
ORIGINAL TRANSMISSION: 1/19-1/20/1984

Villagers re-enacting the English Civil War in 1984 fall under the psychic influence of an evil alien menace. This suspenseful, expertly directed two-parter harkens back to the historical adventures of the Fourth Doctor's early years, and proves that even a shorter outing can deliver plenty of thrills and chills. Excellent turns by Davison, Fielding, and guest stars Keith Jayne and Denis Lill are among the highlights.

A. The Doctor brings Tegan to the village of Little Hodcombe to visit what elderly relative?

B. Sir George (Denis Lill) assigns Tegan what role in the re-enactment?

C. Tinclavic is a metal mined by what alien beings on the planet Raaga?

D. Guest star Denis Lill previously appeared in what Fourth Doctor story about a malevolent alien menacing the occupants of an isolated priory?

E. Which companion had his one and only scene in this story cut from the final edit for time purposes?

"Frontios"

WRITER: Christopher H. Bidmead
DIRECTOR: Ron Jones
STARS: Peter Davison, Janet Fielding, Mark Strickson
ORIGINAL TRANSMISSION: 1/26-2/3/1984

This delightful throwback to the Jon Pertwee era gives "The Caves of Androzani" a run for its money as the best Fifth Doctor tale of all. The Doctor and his companions help human colonists battle subterranean, humanoid gastropods on the planet Frontios. It's debatable who chews more scenery, the overwrought Strickson or visiting villain John Gillett, but there's no question that both play their roles to the hilt. The use of a hat stand as a lethal weapon is classic.

A. What "Frontios" guest star went on to play Mr. Harding in the "Mona Lisa's Revenge" two-parter on *The Sarah Jane Adventures*?

B. Tegan and Turlough steal what object from the research room?

C. Guest star Lesley Dunlop later appears in what Seventh Doctor serial?

D. The Doctor takes the Gravis to what uninhabited planet?

E. The Doctor leaves Plantagenet (Jeff Rawle) what object as a farewell token?

"Resurrection of the Daleks"

WRITER: Eric Saward
DIRECTOR: Matthew Robinson
STARS: Peter Davison, Janet Fielding, Mark Strickson
ORIGINAL TRANSMISSION: 2/8-2/15/1984

Plagued by disease, the Daleks use a time corridor to revive Davros, trap the Doctor, and pave the way for an invasion of Gallifrey. Marvelous performances help ground a story that has a few too many plot threads going at once for its own good. Terry Molloy is utterly brilliant in his first outing as the megalomaniacal Dalek creator last seen in "Destiny of the Daleks." Fielding's exit in the final scene is a heartbreaker.

A. How long has Davros been in cryogenic suspension?

B. Which two companions are not shown during the sequence in which the Doctor undergoes a brain scan?

C. The Daleks plan to use clones of the Doctor and his companions to assassinate the members of what governing body?

D. What glamorous actress, best known for her role in the 1970s musical series *Rock Follies*, plays Styles in this serial?

E. Rodney Bewes co-starred with multi-time *Doctor Who* guest actors Cyril Shaps and Ewen Solon in what 1979 time travel comedy, produced by Disney?

"Planet of Fire"

WRITER: Peter Grimwade
DIRECTOR: Fiona Cumming
STARS: Peter Davison, Mark Strickson, Nicola Bryant
ORIGINAL TRANSMISSION: 2/23-3/2/1984

The Master exploits the religious traditions of the people of Sarn to gain control of the planet's most precious natural resource. The Fifth Doctor's final confrontation with the Master is a slow-paced but enjoyable adventure which benefits greatly from its picturesque locales. Bryant makes quite an impression in her debut, giving new meaning to the phrase "Something for the Dads!" by stripping down to a skimpy bikini moments after first appearing on-screen.

A. Peri (Nicola Bryant) is the first *Doctor Who* companion to hail from what country?

B. To what ancient god do the people of Sarn make their fire sacrifices?

C. Exteriors for this serial were filmed on what scenic island?

D. Which female companion of the 1970s was the first to wear a two-piece swimsuit in an episode of the original series?

E. What short-lived companion made his final physical appearance in this serial?

"The Caves of Androzani"

WRITER: Robert Holmes
DIRECTOR: Graeme Harper
STARS: Peter Davison, Nicola Bryant
ORIGINAL TRANSMISSION: 3/8-3/16/1984

The best writer of the original series and the best director of the 1980s team up to send the Fifth Doctor off in grand fashion with this tense, gritty tale of drugs, duplicity, and death on a remote mining planet. Davison does his best work of the series, sparring skillfully with the story's multiple antagonists and forging a winning chemistry with Bryant. Christopher Gable and John Normington are first-rate villains, while Robert Glenister is fine in double duty as a jaded soldier and his treacherous android doppelganger.

A. How many centiliters of spectrox from his personal stash does the Morgus (John Normington) offer as a gift to the President (David Neal)?

B. What unpleasant-sounding drink is the only known cure for spectrox toxemia?

C. As he is regenerating, the Doctor experiences visions of several of his former companions, as well as what recurring villain?

D. Guest star David Neal previously appeared with Charlton Heston, Christopher Lee, and Diana Rigg in a 1970 film adaptation of what Shakespeare play?

E. John Normington also guest stars in what 2006 episode of *Torchwood*?

(Answers begin on Page 236.)

The Sixth Doctor

1984-1986

COLIN BAKER, A SMALL-SCREEN CHARACTER ACTOR usually cast in villainous roles, hoped to grow into the part of the Doctor when he accepted it in 1984. His unusual approach was to create a Time Lord who was initially easy to dislike and slowly win the audience's favor over time. His stratagem fell through when diminishing ratings and a personal distaste for science fiction prompted BBC Controller Michael Grade to first place the program on an eighteen-month hiatus in 1985, then demand the actor be replaced following the subsequent shortened season.

As the Sixth Doctor, Baker's bombastic voice and extroverted personality helped him steal most of the scenes in which he appeared. Though undeniably pompous and self-absorbed, he was not without courage or compassion when confronting cosmic tyranny. Perhaps the most violent Doctor, he often used weapons to dispatch his enemies. Garish fashion sense and a penchant for theatrical soliloquies only served to make the Sixth Doctor seem even more imperious.

The Sixth Doctor was severely injured and forced to regenerate when the Rani (Kate O'Mara) attacked his TARDIS.

"The Twin Dilemma"

WRITER: Anthony Steven
DIRECTOR: Peter Moffatt
STARS: Colin Baker, Nicola Bryant
ORIGINAL TRANSMISSION: 4/22-4/30/1984

The Doctor and Peri attempt to rescue a pair of brilliant adolescents from the clutches of a slug-like alien conqueror. This one deserves a better reputation than it has garnered over the years, despite some admittedly lackluster set design and rather ineffective cliffhangers. Baker's Doctor may not be very sympathetic at this point, but watching him devour the scenery in great gulps is fun, and the villainous Mestor is a nice throwback to drive-in movie monsters of the 1950s.

A. Guest star Maurice Denham plays Professor Edgeworth, who is actually what aging Time Lord?

B. What one word exclamation does Peri use to describe the Doctor's new wardrobe?

C. Hugo Lang (Kevin McNally) works for what galactic law enforcement agency?

D. How many planets are in the Jacondan solar system?

E. What are the names of the twin actors who play Romulus and Remus?

"Attack of the Cybermen"

WRITER: Paula Woolsey
DIRECTOR: Matthew Robinson
STARS: Colin Baker, Nicola Bryant
ORIGINAL TRANSMISSION: 1/5-1/12/1985

In this busy, violent tale, the Cybermen attempt to reroute Halley's Comet to strike the Earth in 1986, in order to save their home world of Mondas from destruction. The inclusion of the Cyber Controller (Michael Kilgarriff), the mercenary Lytton (Maurice Colbourne), the planet Telos, and the I.M. Foreman scrap yard give this one a nice, nostalgic flavor. Bryant is given little to do but complain, but the rest of the tale works remarkably well.

A. What long-malfunctioning component of the TARDIS does the Doctor attempt to repair in this story, with less-than-spectacular results?

B. Lytton hails from what planetary satellite?

C. Michael Kilgarriff previously appeared as the Cyber Controller in what Second Doctor serial?

D. What do the Cybermen intend to use to destroy the Earth?

E. Prior to playing the mercenary Lytton in two *Doctor Who* serials, Maurice Colbourne starred in the 1981 television adaptation of what classic John Wyndham science-fiction novel?

"Vengeance on Varos"

WRITER: Philip Martin
DIRECTOR: Ron Jones
STARS: Colin Baker, Nicola Bryant
ORIGINAL TRANSMISSION: 1/19-1/26/1985

The Doctor and Peri land on a remote mining planet where torture and public executions are the preferred forms of entertainment. This grim and gritty black comedy pushes the envelope for sadism in what was, at the time, still considered primarily a children's show. Still, it moves along at a nice clip, features some truly campy mad science, and introduces Nabil Shaban's wonderfully slimy scoundrel Sil, one of the best villains in *Doctor Who* history.

A. What precious mineral can only be found on Varos?

B. The rebel Jondar is played by what son of a former James Bond star?

C. Sil represents the interests of what galactic conglomerate?

D. Guest star Steven Yardley previously appeared in what Fourth Doctor serial?

E. Prisoners on Varos are sentenced to navigate the treacherous passages of what sinister structure?

"The Mark of the Rani"

WRITERS: Pip and Jane Baker
DIRECTOR: Sarah Hellings
STARS: Colin Baker, Nicola Bryant
ORIGINAL TRANSMISSION: 2/2-2/9/1985

A renegade Time Lady extracts fluid from the brains of nineteenth-century miners, turning them into violent maniacs. With its modest pacing and quaint, period setting, this one might have been better suited for Peter Davison's Fifth Doctor. As is, it works best when Baker and guest villains Anthony Ainley and Kate O'Mara are trading pointed verbal jabs with one another. Land mines that turn people into trees and a brief appearance by a Tyrannosaurus Rex are nice bonuses.

A. The Rani's TARDIS is disguised as what ordinary object?

B. Guest star Gawn Grainger is married to what actress, who appears as a supremely vain villainess in a pair of new series stories?

C. Kate O'Mara previously appeared in what 1969 episode of the cult series *The Avengers*, opposite the original Master actor, Roger Delgado?

D. The Doctor and Peri meet what renowned English engineer and inventor in this serial?

E. What is the Doctor's wry reply when asked what he and Peri do inside the TARDIS?

"The Two Doctors"

WRITER: Robert Holmes
DIRECTOR: Peter Moffatt
STARS: Colin Baker, Nicola Bryant, Patrick Troughton, Fraser Hines
ORIGINAL TRANSMISSION: 2/16-3/2/1985

The Sixth Doctor teams up with the Second to prevent a brilliant scientist from giving the Sontarans the power of time travel. The cast is exceptional, and the cannibalism theme is suitably grisly to satisfy the bloodthirsty sensibilities of the period. Unfortunately, a bit too much of the three-episode runtime is spent gazing at the scenery in and around

Seville, Spain, where the bulk of the story was shot. The result is an enjoyable but overlong multi-Doctor outing.

A. The Sontarans intend to use Earth as the launching point for an attack on their Rutan enemies in what section of the galaxy?

B. Guest star John Stratton appeared with Patrick Troughton and big-screen *Doctor Who* star Peter Cushing in what 1974 Hammer horror film?

C. James Saxon, who plays the ill-fated Oscar Botcherby here, went on to appear with Timothy Dalton and Jon Pertwee's son, Sean, in what 1999 Hallmark Entertainment mini-series about a legendary *femme fatale*?

D. The Time Lords dispatch the Second Doctor to put an end to the dangerous time travel experiments of what two scientists?

E. The Sixth Doctor angles for what delicious type of fish?

"Timelash"

WRITER: Glen McCoy
DIRECTOR: Pennant Roberts
STARS: Colin Baker, Nicola Bryant
ORIGINAL TRANSMISSION: 3/9-3/16/1985

Without question the most unfairly maligned story in *Doctor Who* history, this unabashedly silly bit of escapism has the Doctor and Peri attempting to avert an intergalactic war on the planet Karfel. It's a throwback to the Saturday matinees and pulp magazines of the 1930s in every way, from the uneven production values to the horribly disfigured villain, to the climactic reveal of Herbert's true identity. If for no other reason, it should be revered for Paul Darrow's sensationally slimy turn as the duplicitous, thoroughly reprehensible Maylin Tekker.

A. What reptilian creatures live in the subterranean caverns of Karfel?

B. Karfel is on the brink of war with what alien race?

C. The Borad (Robert Ashby) attempts to use what chemical to mutate Peri into a perfect mate for him?

D. Which earlier incarnation of the Doctor visited the planet Karfel?

E. Guest star Dean Hollingsworth later appears as a bus conductor in what Seventh Doctor serial?

"Revelation of the Daleks"

WRITER: Eric Saward
DIRECTOR: Graeme Harper
STARS: Colin Baker, Nicola Bryant
ORIGINAL TRANSMISSION: 3/23-3/30/1985

The Doctor and Peri travel to a cosmic funeral home to pay their respects to a deceased friend, only to discover that Davros and his Daleks are running the institution. The final story of Baker's first season is the best, an offbeat and unsettling tale of grave robbing, greed, and galactic overpopulation. As one would expect from director Harper, macabre humor and magnificent performances are the cornerstones of this extremely violent, grisly adventure.

A. Eleanor Bron, who plays Kara here, previously appeared in what Fourth Doctor serial?

B. The Doctor comes to Tranquil Repose to pay last respects to whom?

C. What specialized ammunition can penetrate the armor of a Dalek?

D. Orcini (William Gaunt) is a knight of what celebrated order?

E. Guest star Hugh Walters previously appeared as Runcible in what Fourth Doctor serial?

"The Mysterious Planet"

WRITER: Robert Holmes
DIRECTOR: Nicholas Mallett
STARS: Colin Baker, Nicola Bryant
ORIGINAL TRANSMISSION: 9/6-9/27/1986

In the first segment of the "Trial of a Time Lord" story arc, the prosecuting Valeyard (Michael Jayston) recounts the Doctor's visit to Ravolox, a planet that looks suspiciously like Earth. This lively mystery benefits greatly from the winning performances of guest stars Joan Sims, Tony Selby, and Roger Brierley, as well as a warmer, friendlier relationship between the Doctor and Peri. The opening model shot of a massive Time Lord Space Station is still impressive, a quarter century after this serial first aired.

A. Who composed the new arrangement of the *Doctor Who* opening theme, commissioned specifically for the "Trial of a Time Lord" season?

B. David Rodigan, who plays Broken Tooth here, is the voice of the DJ of what fictional radio station in the video game *Grand Theft Auto: Episodes from Liberty City*?

C. What is Drathro (Roger Brierley)?

D. Sabalom Glitz (Tony Selby) and Dibber (Glen Murphy) have been sent to destroy what machine that provides Drathro with his power?

E. The three sacred books of Marb Station are *Moby Dick* by Herman Melville, *The Water Babies* by Charles Kingsley, and what ornithological manual?

"Mindwarp"

WRITER: Philip Martin
DIRECTOR: Ron Jones
STARS: Colin Baker, Nicola Bryant
ORIGINAL TRANSMISSION: 10/4-10/25/1986

The Doctor and Peri intervene in a bizarre brain surgery experiment on the planet Thoros Beta in this second installment of "The Trial of a Time Lord." Guest stars Nabil Shaban and the bombastic Brian Blessed take turns chewing the scenery, but it's the shocking fate of poor Peri that makes this one utterly unforgettable. The periodic cutaways to the trial are more distracting than intriguing here.

A. Christopher Ryan, who plays Lord Kiv here, later appears in 2008 and 2010 episodes of *Doctor Who*, playing what type of alien menace on both occasions?

B. Sil (Nabil Shaban) is a member of what native Thoros Betan race?

C. Guest star Trevor Laird went on to play the father of what companion of the Tenth Doctor in several episodes of the new series?

D. What alien empire does Yrcanos (Brian Blessed) claim to have conquered on Thordon 2?

E. Guest star Alibe Parsons played a medical technician in what James Cameron-directed science-fiction sequel, released the same year this serial was broadcast?

"Terror of the Vervoids"

WRITERS: Pip and Jane Baker
DIRECTOR: Chris Clough
STARS: Colin Baker, Bonnie Langford
ORIGINAL TRANSMISSION: 11/1-11/22/1986

"The Trial of a Time Lord" continues with this energetic account of deadly, ambulatory plants aboard an intergalactic passenger liner. Langford's spunky Mel has never been highly regarded by fans, but she acquits herself wonderfully here, proving a much better foil for the Doctor's pompous persona than her less assertive predecessor. Nail-biting cliffhangers and claustrophobic sets keep this relatively light-hearted outing from lapsing too far into outright comedy.

A. What drink does Mel insist that the Doctor drink to help reduce his waistline?

B. Guest star Honor Blackman was a regular on what cult spy series from 1962 to 1964?

C. What is the name of the passenger liner besieged by the deadly Vervoids?

D. Pip and Jane Baker wrote the screenplay for what 1969 fantasy film, loosely based on the works of Jules Verne, about an eccentric sea captain and his futuristic vessel?

E. Guest star Bill Fraser previously appeared in "Meglos," as well as the pilot episode of what proposed *Doctor Who* spin-off series?

"The Ultimate Foe"

WRITERS: Robert Holmes, Pip and Jane Baker
DIRECTOR: Chris Clough
STARS: Colin Baker, Bonnie Langford
ORIGINAL TRANSMISSION: 11/29-12/6/1989

The Doctor uncovers the truth behind his trial and pursues his corrupt accuser into the Matrix. Baker delivers his Doctor's famous indictment of his fellow Time Lords with Shakespearean bluster and the harrowing cat-and-mouse game inside a computer-generated reality comes close to matching the grit and suspense of similar sequences in the Fourth Doctor classic "The Deadly Assassin." Geoffrey Hughes, Anthony Ainley, and Tony Selby help close the Sixth Doctor era out in fine style.

A. According to the Doctor, what does it take to be really corrupt?

B. In what 1984 serial does a Time Lord attempt to illegally move an entire planet from its proper place in the cosmos?

C. What sacred object is required to physically gain access to the Matrix?

D. James Bree, who plays the Keeper of the Matrix here, appeared as the Security Chief in what Second Doctor serial?

E. Guest star Geoffrey Hughes provided the speaking voice for which of the Beatles in the 1968 animated fantasy film *Yellow Submarine*?

(Answers begin on Page 240.)

The Seventh Doctor

1987-1989, 1996

THE SEVENTH DOCTOR WAS PORTRAYED BY IRISH ACTOR Sylvester McCoy, whose previous credits include roles in the television series *Big Jim and the Figaro Club* and *Eureka*, and the 1979 film version of *Dracula*. Recently, he was cast in Peter Jackson's two-part big-screen adaptation of J.R.R. Tolkien's *The Hobbit*.

Like Patrick Troughton's Second Doctor before him, McCoy's Time Lord seemed on the surface a funny little man in strange, somewhat ill-fitting clothes, narrowly evading death more through chance than cunning. Beneath that disguise, however, was a deviously clever and manipulative individual, capable of orchestrating complex schemes across the gulf of time and space in order to entrap and defeat his foes.

The Seventh Doctor met an inglorious end when he was gunned down by members of a street gang in the FOX TV movie and regenerated.

"Time and the Rani"

WRITERS: Pip and Jane Baker
DIRECTOR: Andrew Morgan
STARS: Sylvester McCoy, Bonnie Langford
ORIGINAL TRANSMISSION: 9/7-9/28/1987

The Rani hatches a plot to steal the greatest scientific minds in history and take control of time itself. The Seventh Doctor's rather uneven first story benefits greatly from the stellar performances of McCoy and returning *femme fatale* Kate O'Mara, as well as the presence of the bat-like Tetraps. Keff McCulloch's newly arranged, electronic opening theme is a bit jarring at first, but quickly grows on you.

A. Who does the Rani disguise herself as to gain the Doctor's trust?

B. The Doctor says that he and the Rani are both what age?

C. Donald Pickering previously appeared alongside "Time and the Rani" co-star Wanda Ventham in "The Faceless Ones," and played a treacherous prosecutor in what First Doctor serial?

D. Mel professes to be a fan of the works of what English writer and physicist?

E. Andrew Morgan directed what 1980 episode of *Blake's 7*, featuring a guest appearance by Patrick Troughton' son, Michael?

"Paradise Towers"

WRITER: Stephen Wyatt
DIRECTOR: Nicholas Mallett
STARS: Sylvester McCoy, Bonnie Langford
ORIGINAL TRANSMISSION: 10/5-10/26/1987

In this grossly underrated adventure, the Doctor and Mel investigate strange happenings in a dilapidated, twenty-second-century high-rise apartment building. Colorful supporting characters and excellent production design make this darkly comedic outing immensely entertaining even when the Time Lord is off-screen, and the swimming pool sequence is a camp horror classic.

A. What is the name of the Great Architect?

B. Guest star Clive Merrison previously appeared in what Second Doctor serial?

C. Paradise Towers is home to the Kangs, the Caretakers, and what other group?

D. Where is the swimming pool located?

E. Guest star Judy Cornwell appeared alongside Stratford Johns and Edward de Souza in what 1967 comedic film, loosely based on a Jules Verne novel?

"Delta and the Bannermen"

WRITER: Malcolm Kohll
DIRECTOR: Chris Clough
STARS: Sylvester McCoy, Bonnie Langford
ORIGINAL TRANSMISSION: 11/2-11/16/1987

The Doctor and Mel help the last survivor of an alien race defeat the ruthless space pirates who wiped out her species. The broadest and most light-hearted tale of the McCoy era is a loving homage to American science-fiction films of the 1950s. Rock 'n' roll, the space race, and even Disneyland figure into a rather madcap narrative that thoroughly satisfies if viewed in the right frame of mind.

A. The Doctor and Mel visit what fictional Welsh holiday camp, named after a fictional locale in a James Hilton novel, in this serial?

B. What unique accessory to the Doctor's wardrobe makes its debut in this story?

C. Shortly before his death in 1997, guest star Don Henderson appeared with Paul McGann and Bill Nighy in what feature film about the search for fantastic creatures?

D. Guest star Leslie Meadows later appears in an uncredited role as a feline alien in what Seventh Doctor serial?

E. Why do the Doctor and Mel win a free trip to Disneyland?

"Dragonfire"

WRITER: Ian Briggs
DIRECTOR: Chris Clough
STARS: Sylvester McCoy, Bonnie Langford, Sophie Aldred
ORIGINAL TRANSMISSION: 11/23-12/7/1987

McCoy's first season ends on a relative high note as the Doctor and Mel search for a legendary monster in the subterranean caverns of an icy alien world. Tony Selby, Patricia Quinn, and Aldred (as new companion Ace) all deliver winning performances, and the grisly melting head effect in the closing moments still works to this day. If it weren't such a shameless *Alien* rip-off, this one could have been a classic.

A. What is Ace's real first name?

B. Guest star Patricia Quinn is probably best known for playing Magenta in *The Rocky Horror Picture Show* (1975), and what character in its 1981 sequel, *Shock Treatment*?

C. What type of alien, first seen in "The Leisure Hive," appears in the café in Iceworld?

D. Kane (Edward Peel) is from what planet?

E. Guest star Tony Osoba starred in what mid-1980s science-fiction radio drama, which employed stock incidental music from *Alien* (and other theatrical films)?

"Remembrance of the Daleks"

WRITER: Ben Aaronovitch
DIRECTOR: Andrew Morgan
STARS: Sylvester McCoy, Sophie Aldred
ORIGINAL TRANSMISSION: 1/5-10/29/1988

The disparate Dalek plot threads of the Davros era come to a head in this highly regarded tale of two warring factions of the Doctor's greatest enemies vying for control of an ancient Gallifreyan weapon. Set in 1963 London, there are plenty of fan-pleasing nods to the early days of the program, plus a very compelling subplot about racism and a wealth of truly explosive action sequences.

A. The rival Dalek sects are after what ancient Gallifreyan weapon, capable of creating or modifying stars?

B. In how many episodes of the late 1950s comedy series *The Army Game* did guest star Harry Fowler co-star with William Hartnell?

C. Pamela Salem, who plays Dr. Rachel Jensen here, previously appeared in what Fourth Doctor serial?

D. In order to mask the presence of Davros in this serial, Terry Molloy is credited by what pseudonym in the third episode?

E. Guest star Joseph Marcell is best known to U.S. audiences for playing an English butler in what American sitcom of the 1990s?

"The Happiness Patrol"

WRITER: Graeme Curry
DIRECTOR: Chris Clough
STARS: Sylvester McCoy, Sophie Aldred
ORIGINAL TRANSMISSION: 11/2-11/16/1988

The Doctor and Ace land on a dystopian planet where negative emotions have been outlawed. Perhaps a bit too pointed in its skewering of Margaret Thatcher's England for its own good, this visually impressive outing is not as fun as a tale featuring a murderous robot made of candy should be. The performances are excellent across the board, but the story is too short (three episodes) to fully explore its interesting ideas.

A. What former Earth colony is ruled by the tyrannical Helen A (Sheila Hancock)?

B. Helen A's pet, Fifi, is what type of alien creature?

C. What 1931 Herman Hupfeld ballad, best remembered for its inclusion in the classic film *Casablanca*, does the Doctor sing in this serial?

D. Guest player Georgina Hale starred in what 1973 British TV movie about a house run by a sophisticated supercomputer which develops feelings for its female owner?

E. Guest star John Normington appeared in what 1975 science-fiction feature, set in a dystopian future society where athlete Jonathan E (James Caan) is the biggest star of an immensely popular, ultraviolent sports league?

"Silver Nemesis"

WRITER: Kevin Clarke
DIRECTOR: Chris Clough
STARS: Sylvester McCoy, Sophie Aldred
ORIGINAL TRANSMISSION: 11/23-12/7/1988

The twenty-fifth-anniversary serial is another oft-maligned tale from the McCoy era that deserves a much better reputation. Cybermen battle neo-Nazis and a seventeenth-century witch for possession of a powerful ancient weapon. The fact that the plot is essentially a rehash of "Remembrance of the Daleks" does little to diminish the fast-paced fun of this ambitious, all-star outing. The classic Cybermen have never looked better.

A. Though this is the final appearance of living Mondasian Cybermen, the severed head of one appears in what Ninth Doctor story?

B. What mantra is inscribed on the interior wall of Lady Peinforte's tomb?

C. Anton Diffring appeared in the 1966 film adaptation of what classic Ray Bradbury science-fiction novel?

D. What West Sussex historical landmark stands in for Windsor Castle in this serial?

E. The Nemesis statue is composed of what living metal?

"The Greatest Show in the Galaxy"

WRITER: Stephen Wyatt
DIRECTOR: Alan Wareing
STARS: Sylvester McCoy, Sophie Aldred
ORIGINAL TRANSMISSION: 12/14/1988-1/4/1989

The Doctor and Ace discover that a trio of malevolent beings has taken control of the renowned Psychic Circus, with deadly consequences for all who attend. Writer Wyatt's second and final *Doctor Who* story is another macabre masterpiece, loaded with memorable characters and sinister set pieces. Coulrophobic viewers are likely to have nightmares after watching this one.

A. The once traveling Psychic Circus has settled on what planet?

B. Rico Ross, who plays the Ringmaster here, appeared as Captain Frank in what 1997 episode of the American science-fiction series *Babylon 5*?

C. T.P. McKenna appeared alongside "Earthshock" guest star Beryl Reid and "The Ribos Operation" supporting player John Hamill in what 1970 British horror film?

D. The Doctor discovers that what ancient enemies are really in control of the Psychic Circus?

E. Captain Cook (T.P. McKenna) indicates that the planet Anagonia is home to what unusual marine animals?

"Battlefield"

WRITER: Ben Aaronovitch
DIRECTOR: Michael Kerrigan
STARS: Sylvester McCoy, Sophie Aldred, Nicholas Courtney
ORIGINAL TRANSMISSION: 9/6-9/27/1989

The final U.N.I.T. story of the original series is good, nostalgic fun, marred only by the fact that it borrows most of its best tricks from the previous season's "Silver Nemesis." Arthurian knights and a vengeful sorceress battle for possession of the legendary sword Excalibur in modern-day England. Returning guest stars Courtney and Jean Marsh are typically excellent, but it's Marcus Gilbert's intrepid Ancelyn that steals the majority of the scenes.

A. Who is the new commander of the U.N.I.T. forces in the United Kingdom?

B. Marcus Gilbert went on to play another medieval warrior in what 1992 Sam Raimi-directed comedic fantasy film?

C. Guest star June Bland previously appeared in what Fifth Doctor serial?

D. The Brigadier's wife, Doris (played here by Angela Douglas), was first mentioned in what Third Doctor serial?

E. What is Brigadier Lethbridge-Stewart's radio call sign in this serial?

"Ghost Light"

WRITER: Marc Platt
DIRECTOR: Alan Wareing
STARS: Sylvester McCoy, Sophie Aldred
ORIGINAL TRANSMISSION: 10/4-10/18/1989

In this spooky, cerebral tale, the Doctor and Ace investigate evolution and alien beings in a nineteenth-century haunted mansion. Though another case of a few too many compelling ideas and too little time to explore them, the stunning sets and stellar performances make this a highlight in a very solid season. In an era when the Doctor often appeared two steps ahead of everyone else, it's fascinating to watch McCoy's Time Lord slowly, methodically unlocking the dark secrets of the mysterious Gabriel Chase manor.

A. What totem does the Doctor give to Nimrod (Carl Forgione)?

B. Guest star Michael Cochrane is married to actress Belinda Carroll, the sister of what two-time *Doctor Who* guest star?

C. John Hallam, who plays Light here, appeared alongside one-time *Doctor Who* guests Brian Blessed and Timothy Dalton in what 1980 big-screen update of a popular 1930s science-fiction comic strip?

D. What nineteenth-century song, composed by J.F. Mitchell, is performed by Gwendoline (Katharine Schlesinger)?

E. In what year did Ace first visit Gabriel Chase manor?

"The Curse of Fenric"

WRITER: Ian Briggs
DIRECTOR: Nicholas Mallett
STARS: Sylvester McCoy, Sophie Aldred
ORIGINAL TRANSMISSION: 10/25-11/15/1989

The Doctor and Ace battle aquatic, vampire-like creatures on an English military base during World War II. The definitive *Doctor Who* horror story of the 1980s, this atmospheric masterpiece features some of the most unsettling visuals in series' history. Aldred does perhaps her finest work here in a subplot involving Ace's youthful mother. Gorgeous underwater photography and amazing monster make-up are just two of the many highlights of this true classic.

A. What is the Doctor's reply when asked by Kathleen Dudman (Cory Pulman) if he has any family?

B. What was the name of Ace's Computer Studies teacher?

C. Marek Anton plays a Russian soldier here, but appeared as a demonic monster in what earlier Seventh Doctor serial?

D. After facing the vampire-like Haemovores in a small role in this serial, guest star Anne Reid went on to play a bloodsucking Plasmavore in what Tenth Doctor story?

E. What supercomputer is used to decipher both encoded Nazi messages and Viking runes at the base near Maiden's Point?

"Survival"

WRITER: Rona Munro
DIRECTOR: Alan Wareing
STARS: Sylvester McCoy, Sophie Aldred
ORIGINAL TRANSMISSION: 11/22-12/6/1989

Anthony Ainley's Master returns for one last showdown with the Doctor in a series-ending serial about cat-like aliens on a planet on the brink of total destruction. Sadly, this tale's excellent special effects, first-rate performances, and taut pacing are all overshadowed by the inescapable knowledge that it's the final chapter of the original *Doctor Who*. Even in hindsight, McCoy's oft-quoted final words will bring a tear to the eye.

A. "Survival" was the final story of the original series to be transmitted, but which was the last to be recorded?

B. Guest star Kathleen Bidmead's only credited appearance in *Doctor Who* comes in this serial, but her first role in the series was as an Elder of the Tribe of the Free in what Sixth Doctor adventure?

C. The Doctor and Ace encounter the alien kitling in what northern suburb of London?

D. How do the Cheetah People bring humans to their planet?

E. As they return to the TARDIS for the last time, the Doctor tells Ace of "worlds out there where the sky is burning, the sea's asleep and the rivers dream, people made of smoke and cities made of" what?

(Answers begin on Page 242.)

The Eighth Doctor

1996

PAUL MCGANN WAS PRIMARILY A FILM ACTOR PRIOR TO becoming the Doctor, having appeared in *Empire of the Sun*, *Alien 3*, and the 1993 theatrical adaptation of *The Three Musketeers*. In the years since the FOX TV movie came and went, the Liverpudlian actor has continued to work steadily on the silver screen, and has portrayed the Eighth Doctor in numerous audio adventures since 2001.

Because his sole televised adventure depicts the immediate aftermath of a particularly violent "death" and unstable regeneration, the Eighth Doctor remains a bit of an enigma. Through a good portion of his screen time, he is either unconscious or suffering from temporary amnesia. As he recovers, he proves to be soft-spoken but eager for adventure, and extremely courageous. He is also the first Doctor ever to kiss a human female companion on the lips.

The details of the end of the Eighth Doctor's life have yet to be revealed, though it is implied that his regeneration came during or shortly after the Time War between the Time Lords and the Daleks.

"Doctor Who: The Movie"

WRITER: Matthew Jacobs
DIRECTOR: Geoffrey Sax
STARS: Paul McGann, Daphne Ashbrook
ORIGINAL TRANSMISSION: 5/12/1996

The Eighth Doctor's sole outing is a mixed bag of solid production values, strong performances, and inconsistent storytelling. The newly regenerated Time Lord must recover his lost memory in time to prevent the Master from using the Eye of Harmony to steal his remaining regenerations and destroy the Earth. McGann is perfect in the lead role, Roberts much better than given credit for as his arch-nemesis, and the prolonged regeneration sequence unforgettable. Unfortunately, continuity gaffes and a forced romantic subplot keep this otherwise engaging tale from reaching its full potential.

A. Guest star Will Sasso is currently a regular on what CBS situation comedy, starring former *Star Trek* star William Shatner?

B. In which Sixth Doctor serial does the Doctor meet in person the author of the classic science-fiction novel he is reading at the beginning of this story?

C. The Doctor needs to secure what device in order to repair the faulty timing mechanism on the TARDIS?

D. What classic horror film is the morgue attendant (Will Sasso) watching on television as the Doctor regenerates in the next room?

E. Editor Patrick Lussier went on to edit several horror films of the 1990s and 2000s, and directed the 3D remake of what 1980s slasher opus?

F. The Master tells Chang Lee (Yee Jee Tso) that one of the Doctor's previous regenerations was what infamous historical figure?

G. What two other incarnations of the Doctor steal their clothing from hospitals shortly after regenerating?

H. Daphne Ashbrook appears in what 2009 big-screen thriller which shares its title and a few basic plot elements with a 2010 Eleventh Doctor story?

I. The Doctor claims that Leonardo Da Vinci was suffering what physical ailment when he drew the picture which now hangs on Grace's wall?

J. The Master discovers what controversial aspect of the newly regenerated Doctor's physiology?

(Answers on Page 245.)

The Ninth Doctor
2005

LIKE PAUL MCGANN, CHRISTOPHER ECCLESTON WAS AN established film actor when he accepted the lead role in the revived *Doctor Who*. Best known to audiences around the globe for roles in the remake of *Gone in 60 Seconds*, *Shallow Grave*, and *28 Days Later*, he brought an edgy intensity to the part which had been missing since the early days of the William Hartnell era.

The Ninth Doctor was often gruff and impatient, the guilt-ridden sole survivor of an intergalactic war in which he was forced to destroy his own home planet. While he enjoyed music and was not above a little childish frivolity, the pain and anger he felt over the Time War was never far from the surface. This grief also led to a romantic attachment to his human female companion, something no previous iteration of the character had ever developed.

Eccleston left the role after just one season, going on to appear in films like *G.I. Joe: The Rise of Cobra* and *Pan's Labyrinth*, as well as the BBC-produced John Lennon biopic *Lennon Naked*. On-screen, the Ninth Doctor's final act was absorbing the intense radiation of the time vortex in order to save his beloved companion, Rose (Billie Piper).

"Rose"

WRITER: Russell T. Davies
DIRECTOR: Keith Boak
STARS: Christopher Eccleston, Billie Piper, Noel Clarke, Camille Coduri
ORIGINAL TRANSMISSION: 3/26/2005

A bored London shop girl helps the Doctor defeat a new batch of Autons. Told largely from the title character's perspective, this fast-paced outing is a perfect introduction to the Doctor's world for the *Buffy the Vampire Slayer* generation. Eccleston steps into the iconic role with ease, Piper is feisty and endearing, and Clarke and Coduri provide excellent comic relief. The sight of department store mannequins on a killing spree is just as chilling as it was in 1970.

A. The Doctor invokes what intergalactic law in order to gain audience with the Nestene Consciousness?

B. Christopher Eccleston appeared alongside guest star Mark Benton and future *Doctor Who* guest actress Lesley Sharp in what 2003, Russell T. Davies-scripted series about a man who believes he's the reincarnation of Jesus Christ?

C. Mickey (Noel Clarke) is "eaten" by what ordinary plastic object while he waits outside the home of internet Doctor-watcher Clive (Mark Benton)?

D. Rose uses what online search engine to search for information on the Doctor?

E. One of Camille Coduri's earliest film roles came in what 1988 comedy-drama, starring future *Doctor Who* villain Timothy Dalton and three-time guest star Geoffrey Palmer?

"The End of the World"

WRITER: Russell T. Davies
DIRECTOR: Euros Lynn
STARS: Christopher Eccleston, Billie Piper
ORIGINAL TRANSMISSION: 4/2/2005

The tone of the entire Davies era is set with this spectacular cosmic whodunit. The Doctor and his companion investigate sabotage aboard a space station on the eve of Earth's destruction. The visuals are gorgeous and the humor sharp, but it's character moments like Rose realizing she's in over her head and the Doctor coldly dispatching a ruthless villain that make this one a winner.

A. What gift does the Moxx of Balhoon (Jimmy Vee) give to the Doctor?

B. Guest star Yasmin Bannerman later appears as a police detective in what 2006 episode of *Torchwood*?

C. What nonsensical term which implies cheating does the Doctor use to describe his modifications to Rose's cell phone?

D. What group of aliens unleashes the robotic spiders which sabotage the defense systems of Platform 1?

E. Guest star Zoe Wanamaker previously appeared in an uncredited role as a villager in what Fourth Doctor serial?

"The Unquiet Dead"

WRITER: Mark Gatiss
DIRECTOR: Euros Lyn
STARS: Christopher Eccleston, Billie Piper
ORIGINAL TRANSMISSION: 4/9/2005

The Doctor and Rose help Charles Dickens defeat ghost-like aliens and the walking dead in nineteenth-century Cardiff. Simon Callow is wonderful as the weary writer searching for inspiration in this old-fashioned fright fest, featuring future *Torchwood* star Eve Myles as a clairvoyant chambermaid. The ethereal, body-snatching Gelth make quite effective monsters, worthy of a return engagement with the Doctor.

A. How many novels did Charles Dickens complete after meeting the Doctor and Rose in December of 1869?

B. What is the name of Eve Myles' character in this story?

C. What is the name of the funeral parlor that sits right on top of the rift in time and space?

D. The Gelth were transformed into their present gaseous state by what cosmic event?

E. Simon Callow and future *Doctor Who* guest star Michael Gambon previously lent their vocal talents to a 2001 animated version of what Charles Dickens classic?

"Aliens of London/World War Three"

WRITER: Russell T. Davies
DIRECTOR: Keith Boak
STARS: Christopher Eccleston, Billie Piper, Noel Clarke, Camille Coduri
ORIGINAL TRANSMISSION: 4/16-4/23/2005

In the first multi-part adventure of the new series, the Doctor and Rose battle the profiteering alien Slitheen in 10 Downing Street. Though the flatulence humor wears a bit thin, this one still delivers plenty of thrills and chills. A major highlight is Penelope Wilton, playing an unflappable backbench MP destined for much greater things. The return of U.N.I.T. is also a treat, though fans of the original series may have difficulty recognizing the updated version of the elite outfit.

A. The Slitheen are from what planet?

B. What minor character in this story is later revealed to be a member of Torchwood, in a second-season episode of the spin-off series of that same name?

C. Harriet Jones (Penelope Wilton) is the MP for what Parliamentary Constituency?

D. The Doctor tells Rose he is how old?

E. What "Aliens of London/World War Three" guest star is the only performer other than David Tennant to play the same character in each of Russell T. Davies' five years as executive producer, and the only one to appear as the same character in *Doctor Who*, *Torchwood*, and *The Sarah Jane Adventures*?

"Dalek"

WRITER: Robert Shearman
DIRECTOR: Joe Ahearne
STARS: Christopher Eccleston, Billie Piper, Bruno Langley
ORIGINAL TRANSMISSION: 4/30/2005

The Doctor and Rose discover that a collector of alien artifacts has the last living Dalek locked away in his underground bunker. Eccleston is utterly brilliant in the triumphant, terrifying return of the Time Lord's oldest and deadliest enemy — particularly in the closing moments, when the Doctor realizes he has become that which he fears most. If there was any doubt a twenty-first-century *Doctor Who* could work, it was exterminated by this enthralling epic.

A. What does Henry van Statten (Corey Johnson) call his captured Dalek before learning its true name?

B. The Dalek is revived after being touched by whom?

C. From 2000 to 2004, guest star Anna-Louise Plowman had a recurring role on what American science-fiction series about an alien portal to alternate dimensions?

D. Henry van Statten's subterranean base is near what U.S. city?

E. Joe Ahearne created what short-lived 1998 horror series about a secret paramilitary group sanctioned by the Roman Catholic Church to fight vampires?

"The Long Game"

WRITER: Russell T. Davies
DIRECTOR: Brian Grant
STARS: Christopher Eccleston, Billie Piper, Bruno Langley
ORIGINAL TRANSMISSION: 5/7/2005

In this minor diversion, the Doctor and Rose discover that an alien on an orbiting satellite is using television news broadcasts to oppress the human race in the distant future. There are some decent moments of horror, but the real strength of the episode is comedic actor Simon Pegg, who gleefully hams it up as the manipulative monster's right-hand man.

The coda points out quite succinctly that not every human the Doctor meets is suited to be his companion.

A. On what floor of Satellite 5 does the Mighty Jagrafess reside?

B. Suki Cantrell (Anna Maxwell-Martin) is really what wanted member of the dissident group known as the Freedom Fifteen?

C. How many channels are broadcast from Satellite 5?

D. Guest star Christine Adams went on to appear in "The Hanged Man," the penultimate episode of what 2007 American science-fiction series about a reporter who frequently jumps backward in time?

E. Adam receives what surgical enhancement during his visit to Satellite 5?

"Father's Day"

WRITER: Paul Cornell
DIRECTOR: Joe Ahearne
STARS: Christopher Eccleston, Billie Piper, Camille Coduri, Shaun Dingwall
ORIGINAL TRANSMISSION: 5/14/2005

Rose convinces the Doctor to take her back in time to see her deceased father, but intervenes at the last moment and creates a nightmarish alternate timeline. A superlative science-fiction tearjerker, this masterfully acted time travel tale is a fine showcase for the formidable talents of its stars. Piper seldom has trouble turning on the waterworks for a scene, and here her anguish is overwhelming. Dingwall is brilliant in his first *Doctor Who* outing.

A. Shaun Dingwall, who plays Pete Tyler here, appears alongside Freema Agyeman in the first episode of the revival of what 1970s science-fiction series, created by Terry Nation?

B. What day did Pete Tyler die?

C. Julia Joyce, who plays young Rose in this episode, also portrayed younger versions of Billie Piper in *The Ruby in the Smoke* (2006) and what 2007 television adaptation of a Jane Austen novel?

D. After Rose creates a paradox by saving her father's life, what 2002 song is heard playing on Pete's radio in 1987?

E. What flying creatures attack the church where Sarah (Natalie Jones) and Stuart (Christopher Llewellyn) are getting married?

"The Empty Child/The Doctor Dances"

WRITER: Steven Moffat
DIRECTOR: James Hawes
STARS: Christopher Eccleston, Billie Piper, John Barrowman
ORIGINAL TRANSMISSION: 5/21-5/28/2005

Unquestionably the high point of Eccleston's tenure, this insanely creepy story of gas mask-clad monsters terrorizing Londoners during the Blitz remains the standard by which new series tales are judged to this day. Though the introduction of the libidinous Captain Jack Harkness (John Barrowman) pushes the program into unfamiliar, somewhat uncomfortable territory, the performances are all first-rate, and the horror scenes will have even the most seasoned fans shivering in their seats.

A. The medical spacecraft Captain Jack tries to sell Rose and the Doctor originally belonged to what race of alien warriors?

B. What actor plays Jamie, the first human to become a gas mask person?

C. Which of Dr. Constantine's patients has her amputated leg fully restored?

D. Captain Jack uses what alien biotechnology to heal the rope burns on Rose's hands?

E. The Tenth Doctor jokingly asks "Are you my mummy?" while wearing a gas mask in what 2008 story?

"Boom Town"

WRITER: Russell T. Davies
DIRECTOR: Joe Ahearne
STARS: Christopher Eccleston, Billie Piper, John Barrowman, Noel Clarke

The Doctor and his companions discover that a surviving member of the Slitheen family has become the mayor of Cardiff. The weakest episode of the new *Doctor Who* to date is light on both plot and action, but is saved by the excellent performances of Eccleston and returning villainess Annette Badland. The primary purpose of this dialogue-driven story is to set up plot points which figure heavily in the two-part season finale.

A. Blaid Drwg, the name of the nuclear power plant built on the Cardiff rift, is Welsh for what?

B. Guest star William Thomas previously appeared in what Seventh Doctor serial?

C. The Doctor learns that Margaret the Slitheen has been elected Lord Mayor of Cardiff by reading a headline in what newspaper?

D. The TARDIS lands in what public plaza in Cardiff Bay, named after a famous Welsh author?

E. Rose claims that she and the Doctor have visited the Glass Pyramid of Sancleen, as well as what prison planet system?

"Bad Wolf/The Parting of the Ways"

WRITER: Russell T. Davies
DIRECTOR: Joe Ahearne
STARS: Christopher Eccleston, Billie Piper, John Barrowman, Noel Clarke, Camille Coduri

Davies begins his tradition of everything-but-the-kitchen-sink season-enders with this wonky but wildly entertaining tale of reality television, religious fanaticism, and regeneration. The Dalek Emperor has created a new race of Dalek zealots using the human losers of lethal, futuristic game shows broadcast from Satellite 5. The *deus ex machina* resolution feels like a great big cheat, but the acting and the action are uniformly superb, and the final scene is both a heart-wrenching exit for Eccleston and a grand entrance for David Tennant.

A. The Doctor awakens to find himself on the set of a lethal, futuristic version of what reality television show?

B. Guest star Nisha Nayar previously appeared in an uncredited role as a Red Kang in what Seventh Doctor serial?

C. What English actress, who went on to play Tanya Branning on the soap opera *EastEnders*, plays *Big Brother* contestant Lynda Moss?

D. The Doctor attempts to build what device to defeat the Daleks, using the Satellite 5 transmission equipment?

E. Before regenerating, the Doctor indicates that he'd hoped to take Rose to what planet, which shares its name with a scenic Spanish city on Earth?

(Answers begin on Page 245.)

The Tenth Doctor

2005-2010

IT WOULD BE VIRTUALLY IMPOSSIBLE TO OVERSTATE THE global popularity of David Tennant's manic Tenth Doctor, or the impact his charismatic portrayal of the adventurous alien has had on the worldwide success of the program. Just as Tom Baker did in the 1970s, Tennant turned a show with a history of successfully recasting its lead without missing a beat into a genuine star vehicle for one larger-than-life performer. With his toothy grin, intense gaze, wild hair, and seemingly boundless energy, the veteran stage and screen actor created a Doctor whose influence will be felt for generations to come.

The Tenth Doctor was fast-talking, fierce, and funny, an unpredictable individual who could deliver a pun-laden joke, a mouthful of techno-babble, or an impassioned speech against violence with equal conviction. He later became a tragic figure of almost Shakespearean stature, belligerently defying the laws of time for his own ends, only to suffer intense heartache over the consequences. This Doctor genuinely loved his companions, making their inevitable departures that much more painful.

Like his predecessor, the Tenth Doctor sacrificed himself to save a friend, absorbing a lethal dose of radiation from a damaged alien medical device. Before succumbing to regeneration, however, he lamented his "death," and paid brief visits to his past companions.

"Children In Need/The Christmas Invasion"

WRITER: Russell T. Davies
DIRECTORS: Euros Lynn, James Hawes
STARS: David Tennant, Billie Piper, Camille Coduri, Noel Clarke
ORIGINAL TRANSMISSION: 11/18-12/25/2005

The Doctor's unstable regeneration renders him unconscious just before the alien Sycorax take control of one-third of the Earth's population and threaten genocide. The Tenth Doctor era begins with a bang in this rousing, old-fashioned invasion story, which also features the return of Penelope Wilton's popular Harriet Jones (first seen in "Aliens of London/World War III"). While the new Time Lord is out of commission for much of the runtime, the energetic Tennant makes the most of his few waking scenes, and the supporting cast is splendid.

A. What very important thing does the Doctor remember to tell Jackie Tyler (Camille Coduri) and Mickey Smith when he emerges from the crashed TARDIS?

B. Penelope Wilton was a regular on what 1980s British sitcom, alongside former *Doctor Who* villain Richard Briers?

C. What method do the Sycorax use to enslave the minds of one-third of the Earth's human population?

D. In 2008, guest star Anita Briem appeared in a 3D film adaptation of what classic Jules Verne science-fiction novel?

E. What serious injury does the Doctor incur during his duel with the Sycorax Leader?

"New Earth"

WRITER: Russell T. Davies
DIRECTOR: James Hawes
STARS: David Tennant, Billie Piper
ORIGINAL TRANSMISSION: 4/15/2006

Comedic performances rule the day as the Doctor and Rose uncover sinister medical research and an old, body-switching enemy on an Earth-like planet in the distant future. Piper and Tennant both get to ham it up as they take turns being "possessed" by the vengeful Zoe Wanamaker, who caps a second scene-stealing turn as Lady Cassandra with a heartbreaking final scene. This Doctor's admonitions to the last human about accepting death are particularly ironic when viewed in hindsight, considering his own behavior in his final stories, "The Waters of Mars" and 'The End of Time."

A. The Doctor and Rose meet what wise, ancient alien being for the second time on New Earth?

B. What is the name of Lady Cassandra's clone servant, played by Sean Gallagher?

C. Anna Hope reprises her role as the feline nun Novice Hame in what later Tenth Doctor episode?

D. How many diseases are the human clones housed in the hospital's lower level afflicted with?

E. Adjoa Andoh, who plays Sister Jatt here, returns to the series in what recurring role in the next season opener?

"Tooth and Claw"

WRITER: Russell T. Davies
DIRECTOR: Euros Lynn
STARS: David Tennant, Billie Piper
ORIGINAL TRANSMISSION: 4/22/2006

The Doctor and Rose save Queen Victoria from an alien werewolf in nineteenth-century Scotland. Gothic horror stories have long been a staple of *Doctor Who*, and this fast-paced, effects-laden adventure continues that tradition in grand fashion. Pauline Collins makes a fine Victoria, there's a fun reference to a past companion, and Tennant and Piper finally get a chance to fully develop their chemistry together.

A. The Doctor introduces himself to the Queen by what name?

B. The Doctor and Rose are trying to reach 1970s Sheffield to attend a concert by what punk rocker when they land in Victorian Scotland?

C. Pauline Collins previously appeared in what Second Doctor serial, playing a young woman searching for her missing brother?

D. Guest star Ian Hanmore appeared in a 2007 episode of the BBC's "time traveling" cop drama *Life on Mars*, starring what future *Doctor Who* villain actor?

E. Queen Victoria orders the formation of what secretive organization, in order to protect the British Empire from alien attack?

"School Reunion"

WRITER: Toby Whithouse
DIRECTOR: James Hawes
STARS: David Tennant, Billie Piper, Elisabeth Sladen, Noel Clarke, John Leeson
ORIGINAL TRANSMISSION: 4/29/2006

The new and old series meet head-on in this tender, tearful outing. The Doctor, Rose, and Mickey Smith encounter former companions Sarah Jane Smith and K-9 while investigating weird happenings at an elementary school. Anthony Head is magnificent as the malevolent headmaster, but the invasion plot is secondary to the emotionally charged interplay between Tennant, Sladen, and Piper. Clarke and Leeson play exceptionally well off one another in the episode's best comic relief moments.

A. Anthony Head was a regular on what popular American horror series about high-school kids battling monsters and other supernatural threats in a small California town?

B. The Krillitane are using the children of Deffry Vale School to solve what scientific equation?

C. Guest star Lucinda Dryzek appeared briefly in the 2003 supernatural adventure film *Pirates of the Caribbean: The Curse of the Black Pearl*, playing a younger version of the character essayed by what Oscar-nominated actress?

D. The Doctor infiltrates the school by posing as John Smith, teacher of what elementary subject?

E. Sarah reveals that the Doctor left her in what Scottish city after their last adventure?

"The Girl in the Fireplace"

WRITER: Steven Moffat
DIRECTOR: Euros Lynn
STARS: David Tennant, Billie Piper, Noel Clarke
ORIGINAL TRANSMISSION: 5/6/2006

The Doctor meets and falls for Madame de Pompadour in this unusual but mature and affecting foray into period romance. Tennant and guest star Sophia Myles were dating during production, so the on-screen romantic sparks were real enough to offset the story's more conventional elements, which include a claustrophobic derelict spaceship filled with time-space portals and an army of chilling clockwork men. One very funny highlight involves the Doctor pretending to be severely inebriated in order to trick the metal monsters.

A. Sophia Myles played the Lady Penelope Creighton-Ward in the 2004 live-action adaptation of what iconic Gerry Anderson marionette series?

B. The Clockwork Men believe that Reinette must be how old before her brain will be compatible with their ship's systems?

C. The real Madame de Pompadour died of what ailment at the age of forty-two?

D. Frequent *Doctor Who* monster actor Paul Kasey, who appears as a Clockwork Man here, plays a werewolf in several episodes of what Toby Whithouse-created horror series on BBC Three?

E. What cosmic event damaged the Clockwork Men's ship, prompting them to seek human organs to replace the broken components?

"Rise of the Cybermen/The Age of Steel"

WRITER: Tom MacRae
DIRECTOR: Graeme Harper
STARS: David Tennant, Billie Piper, Noel Clarke, Camille Coduri, Shaun Dingwall
ORIGINAL TRANSMISSION: 5/13-5/20/2006

Director Harper brings plenty of dark humor and pathos to this exceptionally well-crafted tale of a new race of Cybermen birthed on a parallel Earth. With its stunning reinvention of a classic *Doctor Who* monster, some overt references to the timeless Second Doctor epic "The Invasion," and plenty of powerful moments for Piper and Clarke as their characters encounter alternate versions of loved ones long lost in our world, this grim two-parter stands out as a highlight of the Tennant era.

A. What is the name of the parallel Earth version of Mickey Smith?

B. Guest star Roger Lloyd Pack's character in the 2005 film *Harry Potter and the Goblet of Fire* is murdered by his own son, who is played by what actor?

C. The Doctor and his companions realize they are on a parallel Earth when they see that the otherwise ordinary-looking sky is filled with what?

D. Colin Spaull, who plays Mr. Crane here, previously appeared in what Graeme Harper-directed Sixth Doctor serial about humans being converted into alien monsters?

E. What is the parallel Earth Rose Tyler?

"The Idiot's Lantern"

WRITER: Mark Gatiss
DIRECTOR: Euros Lynn
STARS: David Tennant, Billie Piper
ORIGINAL TRANSMISSION: 5/27/2006

An electronic alien uses television to feed on the electrical activity of human brains on the eve of the coronation of Queen Elizabeth II. An admittedly lesser effort, this one benefits greatly from the undeniable chemistry between Tennant and Piper, and the sinister scenes of face-less human victims being rushed away by tight-lipped police officers. An interrogation scene in which the Doctor shifts effortlessly from being the prime suspect to heading the investigation is nicely reminiscent of a similar bit in the Fourth Doctor classic "The Talons of Weng-Chiang."

A. The Doctor is trying to take Rose to a concert by what legendary musician when he inadvertently lands the TARDIS in Muswell Hill?

B. The Wire is using television sets built and sold by what small electronics firm?

C. Extra Laura Phillipart portrays Jasmine Pearce in what 2006 episode of *Torchwood*?

D. The Doctor traps the Wire on what now-obsolete recording medium?

E. Guest star Debra Gillett co-starred with Paul McGann's older brother, Joe, in the 1992 animated adaptation of what Terry Pratchett novel?

"The Impossible Planet/The Satan Pit"

WRITER: Matt Jones
DIRECTOR: James Strong
STARS: David Tennant, Billie Piper
ORIGINAL TRANSMISSION: 6/3-6/10/2006

A dark, oppressive two-parter which features the debut of the alien Ood, and pits the last of the Time Lords against the ultimate evil. Assisting in the investigation of a planet which is somehow resisting the gravitational pull of a nearby black hole, the Doctor and Rose come face-to-face with a malevolent beast which may be the devil himself. Marred only by the Doctor's slightly skewed priorities in the climactic confrontation (he's more concerned about Rose than safety of the rest of the universe), this one packs a serious punch.

A. Guest star Shaun Parkes co-starred with David Tennant in the 2005 serial *Casanova*, and appeared with Billie Piper in what 2004 film?

B. What is the name of the planet under investigation by the crew of the Sanctuary Base?

C. What ill-fated officer was in command of the Sanctuary Base prior to the field promotion of Zachary Cross Flane (Shaun Parkes)?

D. Guest star Claire Rushbrook appeared in the *Doctor Who* celebrity episode of what popular UK game show, which was spoofed in the previous season's two-part finale?

E. Guest star Danny Webb previously appeared with Paul McGann in *Alien 3* (1992), and in the 1985 television adaptation of Karl Wittlinger's *Do You Know the Milky Way?* with what former *Doctor Who* star?

"Love & Monsters"

WRITER: Russell T. Davies
DIRECTOR: Dan Zeff
STARS: Marc Warren, Camille Coduri, Shirley Henderson, David Tennant, Billie Piper
ORIGINAL TRANSMISSION: 6/17/2006

A lonely loser finds happiness when he joins a group of would-be investigators searching for the Doctor, but soon runs afoul of a man-eating alien monster (Peter Kay). This unusual, oft-maligned tale relegates Tennant and Piper to the background, giving guest star Warren and recurring player Coduri a chance to truly shine. They do not disappoint, lending considerable emotional depth to an intentionally light, airy plot. Despite its inherent silliness, this unique story of real people seeking solace in flights of fancy is rather difficult to dislike when taken in the right spirit.

A. What does the acronym LINDA stand for?

B. According to the headline on the Abzorbaloff's copy of *The Daily Mirror*, what politician leads the pre-election polls for British Prime Minister by sixty-four percent?

C. Elton (Marc Warren) witnesses the Doctor and Rose fleeing from what alien monster in an abandoned warehouse?

D. Marc Warren previously appeared as a murderous immortal in what 1996 episode of the syndicated adventure program *Highlander: The Series*, alongside Fine Young Cannibals vocalist Roland Gift?

E. The Abzorbaloff hails from what planet?

"Fear Her"

WRITER: Matthew Graham
DIRECTOR: Euros Lynn
STARS: David Tennant, Billie Piper
ORIGINAL TRANSMISSION: 6/24/2006

In another tale of spousal/parental abuse, monsters in suburbia, and the impact of a major historical event on the lives of everyday people, a lonely little girl's drawings come to life and threaten the entire world. The undeniable fact that it's essentially a twenty-first-century rehash of "The Idiot's Lantern" has severely damaged this well-acted story's reputation, but it's not without memorable moments. The best scene has the Doctor and Rose battling a murderous, living squiggle.

A. The fictitious cul-de-sac where Chloe Webber (Abisola Agbaje) lives is named after what real-life British Olympic athlete?

B. Chloe is possessed by what endothermic alien being?

C. Guest star Tim Faraday played a character called "The Cleaner" in several 2008 episodes of what ITV science-fiction series?

D. What real-life BBC News journalist provides the television commentary for the 2012 Olympic Games in this episode?

E. Nina Sosanya, who plays Trish Webber in this story, previously appeared with David Tennant in what three-part television serial, written by Russell T. Davies?

"Army of Ghosts/Doomsday"

WRITER: Russell T. Davies
DIRECTOR: Graeme Harper
STARS: David Tennant, Billie Piper, Noel Clarke, Camille Coduri, Shaun Dingwall
ORIGINAL TRANSMISSION: 7/1-7/8/2006

In this tour de force finale to the new series' second season, the Doctor and Rose infiltrate the mysterious Torchwood Institute to uncover the secret of silent, ghost-like beings which have been regularly appearing on contemporary Earth since their last visit. The dramatic thrust of the story is Piper's heart-wrenching exit, but there is plenty of spectacle, action, and fan-pleasing fun (including a long-anticipated meeting between two of the Time Lord's oldest and deadliest foes) to keep things moving along until the tearjerking final moments.

A. What two future companion actresses make their *Doctor Who* debuts in this story, playing an ill-fated Torchwood employee and an angry bride, respectively?

B. What can the Doctor see with his 3D glasses?

C. "Doomsday" is the first episode in the history of *Doctor Who* in which what two popular alien enemies appear on-screen together?

D. Rose and her family follow the Doctor's voice to what remote Norwegian beach on the parallel Earth?

E. The Genesis Ark was originally built by what alien beings?

"The Runaway Bride"

WRITER: Russell T. Davies
DIRECTOR: Euros Lyn
STARS: David Tennant, Catherine Tate
ORIGINAL TRANSMISSION: 12/25/2006

On Christmas Eve, the Doctor and a crass, loudmouthed bride-to-be (Tate) must save the Earth from a spider-like alien and her brood of flesh-eating offspring. A largely comedic effort, showcasing the brilliant Tate in a role that no one at the time could have predicted would so profoundly impact the Tenth Doctor's tenure. Sarah Parish overdoes it a bit as the bellicose Racnoss, but scenes of the TARDIS chasing a car down a crowded motorway and a star-shaped spacecraft attacking London are great fun.

A. Where does the Doctor first meet Donna Noble?

B. Donna is a temp at what security firm, owned by the now-defunct Torchwood Institute?

C. Guest star Krystal Archer briefly reprises her role as Donna's nemesis, Nerys, in what later Tenth Doctor story?

D. The Doctor uses what device to re-direct the TARDIS when the Empress of the Racnoss attempts to summon the ship to her lair?

E. What "The Runaway Bride" guest star died shortly after reprising his role in the 2008 season opener, forcing the production team to retool the series to include Bernard Cribbins as Donna's grandfather, Wilfred Mott?

"Smith and Jones"

WRITER: Russell T. Davies
DIRECTOR: Charles Palmer
STARS: David Tennant, Freema Agyeman, Adjoa Andoh, Gugu Mbatha-Raw, Reggie Yates, Trevor Laird
ORIGINAL TRANSMISSION: 3/31/2007

Tennant's second full year as the Doctor kicks off with an impressive tale of an Earth hospital mysteriously transported to the surface of the moon. The stunning Agyeman is quite likable as the resourceful young medical student, Martha Jones, while the rhinoceros-like Judoon bring a nice mixture of brute menace and Douglas Adams-style absurdity to the proceedings.

A. What alien life form are the Judoon searching for?

B. The Judoon mark the hands of individuals identified as human with what symbol?

C. Freema Agyeman stars alongside former *Doctor Who* villains Dervla Kirwan and Paul Darrow, and Fifth Doctor actor Peter Davison, in what British adaptation of a long-running American primetime drama?

D. The Doctor tells Martha that he played with bricks composed of what dangerous material when he was in the nursery?

E. Clive Jones' buxom blonde girlfriend is played by what British actress?

"The Shakespeare Code"

WRITER: Gareth Roberts
DIRECTOR: Charles Palmer
STARS: David Tennant, Freema Agyeman
ORIGINAL TRANSMISSION: 4/7/2007

Alien witches are determined to use the words of brilliant playwright William Shakespeare to open a portal into this reality, through which the rest of their kind can invade the Earth. A rather silly and somewhat self-indulgent historical that benefits immensely from the contributions of the underappreciated Agyeman. Martha's fears about public reaction to her skin color in Elizabethan England, her unrequited love for the Doctor, and her flirtatious banter with the Bard (Dean Lennox Kelly) make this one a worthwhile, if minor, diversion.

A. The Doctor and Martha land in England in what year?

B. Guest star Chris Larkin is the eldest son of Dame Maggie Smith, who teaches students the magical arts in what popular fantasy film series?

C. Martha originates what traditional chant following the performance of *Love's Labours Lost*?

D. According to the Doctor, Elizabethan England has recycling, water cooler chatter, public entertainment, and what environmental phenomenon (inspired by the warnings of a fire-and-brimstone street prophet)?

E. Angela Pleasence, who appears here as Queen Elizabeth I, is the daughter of what legendary British actor?

"Gridlock"

WRITER: Russell T. Davies
DIRECTOR: Richard Clark
STARS: David Tennant, Freema Agyeman
ORIGINAL TRANSMISSION: 4/14/2007

Agyeman again shines in this effects-driven return to New Earth, where thousands of flying vehicles are caught in a perpetual state of gridlock on a futuristic motorway. Highlights include the final appearance of the enigmatic Face of Boe, the return of some long-forgotten original series monsters, a cryptic message about the future, and a solid guest cast, but it's Martha's assertiveness at the end that leaves the strongest impression in this Seventh Doctor-style dystopian drama.

A. What monstrous creatures, first introduced in a Second Doctor serial, reside beneath the crowded skyways of New Earth?

B. What is the name of the mood-altering chemical that mutated into a virus and killed the surface population of the planet?

C. What Irish comedic actor appears here as the cat-like Brannigan?

D. According to Novice Hame, how long did it take for the virus to wipe out life on the surface of New Earth?

E. Guest star Struan Rodger does not provide the voice of the Face of Boe in which of the three stories featuring the enigmatic alien?

"Daleks in Manhattan/Evolution of the Daleks"

WRITER: Helen Raynor
DIRECTOR: James Strong
STARS: David Tennant, Freema Agyeman
ORIGINAL TRANSMISSION: 4/21-4/28/2007

The heavy-handed Dalek tales of the previous two seasons give way to this raucous pulp piece about evil aliens exploiting the misfortunes of Depression-era Americans to facilitate some good, old-fashioned mad science. With gum-chewing showgirls, mutant pig-men, a hideous human-Dalek hybrid, and a harrowing climax atop the Empire State Building, this is classic Saturday matinee science-fiction, meant to be enjoyed without too much analysis. A throwback to the *Doctor Who* of old, guaranteed to please fans of the Troughton and Pertwee eras.

A. Leggy guest star Miranda Raison previously appeared in "Castle Keep," a 2001 episode of what Canadian horror series hosted by one-time *Doctor Who* villain actor Eric Roberts?

B. The Doctor and Martha arrive in New York from what city?

C. Which member of the Cult of Skaro has its DNA combined with that of Mr. Diagoras (Eric Loren) to create a human-Dalek hybrid?

D. Guest star Hugh Quarshie played Captain Panaka in which installment of the *Star Wars* prequel trilogy?

E. In what First Doctor serial do the Daleks visit the Empire State Building?

"The Lazarus Experiment"

WRITER: Stephen Greenhorn
DIRECTOR: Richard Clark
STARS: David Tennant, Freema Agyeman, Adjoa Andoh, Gugu Mbatha-Raw, Reggie Yates
ORIGINAL TRANSMISSION: 5/5/2007

The Doctor and Martha intervene when a brilliant scientist's age-regression machine turns him into a marauding, scorpion-like monster. Frequent *Doctor Who* writer Mark Gatiss goes before the cameras and turns in a winning performance as the ambitious, ill-fated Professor Lazarus in this *Frankenstein*-inspired tale. The computer-generated monster doesn't quite work, but the action is fast and furious, and many important plot points for the season are established here.

A. How much time has passed since her departure in the TARDIS when Martha returns to contemporary Earth?

B. How many *Doctor Who* writers have also acted in episodes of the series?

C. What article of clothing does the Doctor say always causes trouble when he wears it?

D. Lucy O'Connell, who plays a party guest here, appeared as a nurse in what 2005 comedic film alongside *Doctor Who* guest stars Lynda Baron, Honor Blackman, and Peter Bowles, and alternate Ninth Doctor Richard E. Grant?

E. Professor Lazarus takes shelter inside what historic London landmark?

"42"

WRITER: Chris Chibnall
DIRECTOR: Graeme Harper
STARS: David Tennant, Freema Agyeman
ORIGINAL TRANSMISSION: 5/19/2007

Though it covers much of the same ground as the previous year's "The Impossible Planet/The Satan Pit" and the Fourth Doctor epic "Planet of Evil," this nail-biting, real-time potboiler stands out for Harper's solid direction and strong performances by the leads. The Doctor and Martha answer a distress call from a spacecraft careening out of control toward a blazing star. Tennant is utterly terrifying in the scenes in which the Time Lord is enslaved by an unseen alien presence bent on murdering everyone onboard.

A. The distress call picked up by Martha's modified cell phone comes from what deep space vessel?

B. How are Korwin (Matthew Chambers), who is infected by the mysterious illness, and Captain McDonnell (Michelle Collins) related?

C. The mysterious woman who monitors Francine Jones' telephone conversations with Martha is played by what South African-born actress?

D. The title of this episode refers to what?

E. Michelle Collins was a regular on what late 1980s British sitcom, the second season of which was produced and directed by "The Invisible Enemy" director Derrick Goodwin?

"Human Nature/The Family of Blood"

WRITER: Paul Cornell
DIRECTOR: Charles Palmer
STARS: David Tennant, Freema Agyeman
ORIGINAL TRANSMISSION: 5/26-6/2/2007

To escape from bloodthirsty aliens, the Doctor uses Gallifreyan technology to become human and hide out on Earth in 1913. Writer Cornell's own thought-provoking novel of pre-World War I England becomes a showcase for a truly exquisite performance by Tennant, as a seemingly ordinary man haunted by visions of a strange world he can't comprehend. Racism and romance both factor in, along with some genuinely unsettling living scarecrows. Horrifying and heartbreaking, this acclaimed tale represents contemporary television drama at its absolute best.

A. What alien device does the Doctor use to rewrite his DNA and become human?

B. In what ordinary device does the Doctor store his consciousness when he becomes human?

C. What title does John Smith give to the diary in which he records his fantastic dreams?

D. Guest star Jessica Hynes co-wrote and starred in what science-fiction comedy series, alongside one-time *Doctor Who* villain Simon Pegg?

E. Harry Lloyd, who plays Baines in this story, is the great-great-great-grandson of what legendary writer, who the Ninth Doctor met during a visit to nineteenth-century Wales?

"Blink"

WRITER: Steven Moffat
DIRECTOR: Hettie MacDonald
STARS: Carrie Mulligan, Finlay Robertson, David Tennant, Freema Agyeman
ORIGINAL TRANSMISSION: 6/9/2007

Before becoming a celebrated big-screen star, Mulligan took center stage in this much-lauded adaptation of a 2006 short story by Moffat. The Doctor, stranded in the past without his TARDIS, uses messages hidden on DVDs to warn a young woman about malevolent, living statues. Mulligan is amiable and sympathetic, and the Weeping Angels stand alongside the Ood and the new Cybermen as the most memorable monsters of the revived series. The closing montage will send chills up your spine.

A. Hettie MacDonald is the first female director to helm a *Doctor Who* episode since Sarah Hellings directed what Sixth Doctor serial?

B. Sally finds what object hanging from the hand of an angel statue in the Wester Drumlins house?

C. What unusual method do the Weeping Angels use to kill their victims?

D. The Doctor and Martha are trapped in what year?

E. Guest star Richard Cant is the son of actor and television presenter Brian Cant, who appeared in which two 1960s *Doctor Who* serials?

"Utopia / The Sound of Drums / Last of the Time Lords"

WRITER: Russell T. Davies
DIRECTORS: Graeme Harper, Colin Teague
STARS: David Tennant, Freema Agyeman, John Barrowman, Adjoa Andoh, Gugu Mbatha-Raw, Trevor Laird, Reggie Yates
ORIGINAL TRANSMISSION: 6/16-6/23-6/30/2007

After finding the Master alive and well in the far distant future, the Doctor, Martha, and Captain Jack Harkness follow the evil Time Lord back to contemporary Earth, where they discover that he's been elected to Britain's highest office. Mesmerizing performances by Derek Jacobi and John Simm (both playing the Master), cinematic visuals, and solid turns by the supporting players greatly aid a story that's overstocked with painfully obvious Christ metaphors. Tennant's last two scenes with Simm are topnotch, foreshadowing their epic final confrontation in "The End of Time."

A. The letters of Professor Yana's last name are an acronym of what statement made by the Face of Boe in an earlier story?

B. The Master uses what satellite network to telepathically influence voters to vote for Harold Saxon?

C. Guest star Colin Stinton went on to appear in what factual 2009 TV movie about the build-up to the Apollo 11 lunar landing?

D. What rock star wife and television talent show judge appears as herself in this story, endorsing Harold Saxon for Prime Minister?

E. What wholly fictitious alien race does Prime Minister Harold Saxon claim to have made contact with?

"Time Crash/Voyage of the Damned"

WRITERS: Steven Moffat, Russell T. Davies
DIRECTORS: Graeme Harper, James Strong
STARS: David Tennant, Peter Davison, Kylie Minogue, Bernard Cribbins
ORIGINAL TRANSMISSION: 11/16-12/25/2007

Doctor Who does *The Poseidon Adventure* in this action-packed bit of high-tech fluff. After briefly crossing paths with an earlier version of himself, the Doctor must stop the interstellar passenger liner *Titanic* from crashing to Earth. Davison and Tennant are fantastic in Moffat's sweet, sentimental multi-Doctor short, while Minogue's starry-eyed Astrid is the highlight of Davies' loving homage to 1970s disaster films.

A. The Fifth Doctor initially worries that the Tenth, who he has never met before, may be a member of what oddball group of fans-turned-investigators?

B. Bernard Cribbins' starred in which of the 1960s *Doctor Who* theatrical films?

C. Jessica Martin, who provides the voice of Queen Elizabeth II in this story, previously appeared in what Seventh Doctor serial?

D. The diminutive alien Bannakaffalatta is played by what actor, who has also portrayed a Graske, a Groske, a Slitheen, the Moxx of Balhoon, and a Space Pig in various episodes of *Doctor Who* and *The Sarah Jane Adventures*?

E. The ill-informed historian Mr. Copper (Clive Swift) is said in what later Tenth Doctor adventure to have designed a "sub-wave" communications network instrumental in thwarting a Dalek plot to destroy the universe?

"Partners in Crime"

WRITER: Russell T. Davies
DIRECTOR: James Strong
STARS: David Tennant, Catherine Tate, Bernard Cribbins
ORIGINAL TRANSMISSION: 4/5/2008

The Doctor and an old acquaintance cross paths while investigating a new diet drug that converts human fat into living, alien creatures. In Donna Noble, the Tenth Doctor finally gets a companion strong enough to challenge him for the spotlight at every turn, and their unlikely pairing pays immediate dividends for viewers. Though lighter than air, this fantastic farce is among the best season openers in the program's long history.

A. What company is under investigation by Donna and the Doctor?

B. The Doctor tells Donna he's looking for what in a traveling companion?

C. According to Miss Foster, what happened to the breeding planet of the Adipose?

D. What former companion actress has a brief cameo in this episode?

E. Guest star Sue Kelvin previously appeared in "Back in the Red: Part 2," a 1999 episode of what long-running science-fiction comedy series?

"The Fires of Pompeii"

WRITER: James Moran
DIRECTOR: Colin Teague
STARS: David Tennant, Catherine Tate
ORIGINAL TRANSMISSION: 4/12/2008

Tate proves she's much more than just a comedic powerhouse in an energetic, emotional tale of the impending eruption of Mount Vesuvius. Packed with deliberate anachronisms and winking asides, this throwback to the historical serials of the Hartnell era is ultimately about the conflict between compassion and duty. Donna's desperate pleas to the reluctant Doctor to save the ill-fated citizens of Pompeii are truly heartbreaking.

A. What future companion actress appears as a soothsayer in this story?

B. What rock-like aliens secretly dwell in the crater of Mount Vesuvius?

C. Phil Davis, who plays Lucius Petrus Dextrus here, appeared alongside Paul McGann in what 1992 science-fiction film?

D. The Doctor uses what unusual weapon to ward off the fiery aliens?

E. Guest star Victoria Wicks went on to appear in three episodes of the 2009 ITV drama series *Collision*, playing the wife of a character portrayed by what former *Doctor Who* star?

"Planet of the Ood"

WRITER: Keith Temple
DIRECTOR: Graeme Harper
STARS: David Tennant, Catherine Tate
ORIGINAL TRANSMISSION: 4/19/2008

The Doctor and Donna visit the Ood-Sphere, where Ood being cultivated as servants are succumbing to a disease that turns them homicidal. Excellent performances by the entire cast and sharp direction by Harper make this *Conquest of the Planet of the Apes*-inspired action piece a deserving fan favorite. The final fate of the villainous Klineman Halpen (Tim McInnerny) is both exceptionally grisly and immensely gratifying.

A. In what year do the Doctor and Donna arrive on the Ood-Sphere?

B. The Ood adapted with a "classic comedy voice" utters a catchphrase from what long-running U.S. sitcom?

C. Tim McInnerny played novelist Franz Kafka, author of *The Metamorphosis*, in a 1993 episode of what television adventure series, based on a blockbuster big-screen franchise?

D. Klineman Halpen regularly drinks tonic to combat what ailment?

E. Guest star Adrian Rawlins plays the father of what character in the *Harry Potter* film series?

"The Sontaran Stratagem/The Poison Sky"

WRITER: Helen Raynor
DIRECTOR: Douglas Mackinnon
STARS: David Tennant, Catherine Tate, Freema Agyeman, Bernard Cribbins
ORIGINAL TRANSMISSION: 4/26-5/3/2008

For the second straight year, writer Raynor revives a classic *Doctor Who* monster with a plot that's more pulp escapism than cerebral science fiction. The Sontarans use a common automobile guidance system to poison Earth's atmosphere, making it more suitable for them. A fun, fast-paced return to the U.N.I.T.-based stories of the 1970s, marred only by the rather unimpressive new-look Sontarans. Their "Sontar-ha!" war chant is, however, quite infectious.

A. Though it is not mentioned in this story, Martha Jones briefly worked for what group of paranormal investigators before joining U.N.I.T. as a Medical Officer?

B. This story marks the return of what impressive U.N.I.T. vessel, introduced in the previous season's three-part finale?

C. Who developed the ATMOS navigation system?

D. Guest star Bridget Hodgson appeared as a Nazi scientist in what 2004 action film, based on a popular Dark Horse Comics series?

E. Douglas Mackinnon directed the first three episodes of what 2007 horror serial, written by Steven Moffatt, and starring one-time *Doctor Who* guest players Paterson Joseph and Michelle Ryan?

"The Doctor's Daughter"

WRITER: Stephen Greenhorn
DIRECTOR: Alice Troughton
STARS: David Tennant, Catherine Tate, Freema Agyeman
ORIGINAL TRANSMISSION: 5/10/2008

On a war-ravaged planet, the Doctor's DNA is used to create a youthful female clone. This is a grossly underrated episode with a great climactic twist, a winning turn by the lovely Georgia Moffett (in the title role), and a positively bravura performance from Tennant. The only weak point is the very last scene, which feels like a bit of a cop-out after all the heart-wrenching emotion that precedes it.

A. Georgia Moffett is the daughter of what former *Doctor Who* star?

B. In January 2011, the British newspaper *The Telegraph* announced that Moffett was engaged to marry what former *Doctor Who* star?

C. The Doctor and his companions encounter the Hath and their human enemies on what desolate world?

D. The humans and the Hath are at war over what mysterious object?

E. Donna gives the Doctor's daughter what name, based on the Doctor's description of her as a generated anomaly?

"The Unicorn and the Wasp"

WRITER: Gareth Roberts
DIRECTOR: Graeme Harper
STARS: David Tennant, Catherine Tate
ORIGINAL TRANSMISSION: 5/17/2008

The Doctor and Donna help legendary mystery writer Agatha Christie solve a real-life whodunit involving a stolen necklace, several murders, and a giant, alien wasp. Loaded with references to Christie's works, this comedic episode is heavy on slapstick silliness and light on substance. Though not a favorite among fans, it's a fun and frivolous romp, bolstered by an excellent guest cast and a generous helping of Tennant-Tate banter.

A. Guest star Felicity Kendall co-starred with one-time *Doctor Who* villain Richard Briers in what late 1970s sitcom about a married couple who decide to become entirely self-sufficient?

B. The giant wasp is what type of alien being?

C. The Doctor is searching for what Frankish ruler, who has been "kidnapped by an insane computer," in the flashback sequence?

D. Christopher Benjamin, who plays Colonel Hugh in this story, portrayed Sir Keith Gold in what Third Doctor serial?

E. Following her disappearance in December of 1926, the real Agatha Christie was found at the Swan Hydropathic Hotel in Yorkshire, registered under what alias?

"Silence in the Library/Forest of the Dead"

WRITER: Steven Moffat
DIRECTOR: Euros Lynn
STARS: David Tennant, Catherine Tate
ORIGINAL TRANSMISSION: 5/31-6/7/2008

This dark, atmospheric epic introduces the enigmatic River Song (Alex Kingston), and gives Tate yet another chance to show off her marvelous acting range. The Doctor, Donna, and a group of Earth explorers battle microscopic, flesh-eating aliens in a deserted, planet-sized cosmic library. A spine-tingling horror show from beginning to end, this one also features some truly affecting dramatic moments. The tragic "ghosting" sequence alone would have made this an instant classic, but Donna's alternate life outside the Library elevates the emotion to a new level.

A. Before returning as River Song in Matt Smith's first season of *Doctor Who*, Alex Kingston had a recurring role on what short-lived U.S. science-fiction series?

B. What tiny, carnivorous creatures prowl the shadows of the Library?

C. How many members of Professor Song's expedition are named Dave?

D. Tallulah Riley, whose character here dies and is "resurrected" in a computer-created reality, appears as a psychological projection in what 2010 blockbuster film?

E. River Song claims her sonic screwdriver was a gift from whom?

"Midnight"

WRITER: Russell T. Davies
DIRECTOR: Alice Troughton
STARS: David Tennant, Catherine Tate
ORIGINAL TRANSMISSION: 6/14/2008

In this futuristic take on the classic *Twilight Zone* episode "The Monsters Are Due on Maple Street," the Doctor and a group of galactic tourists are terrorized by an unseen alien force on a resort planet. Brutally tense and claustrophobic, this outing relies more on frantic performances and frayed nerves than fancy visuals for its many effective scares. Watch the shuttle monitor screen for a foreshadowing cameo.

A. The Doctor takes the shuttle in order to see what landmark on the planet Midnight?

B. Dee Dee (Ayesha Antoine) informs the Doctor that she's written a paper on what "lost" moon?

C. Which member of the tour group is possessed by the unseen force outside the shuttle?

D. Aside from their association with *Doctor Who*, how are guest star David Troughton and director Alice Troughton related?

E. Tony Bluto, who plays Driver Joe here, appeared as a dockyard engineer in what 2006 British TV movie about a haunted submarine?

"Turn Left"

WRITER: Russell T. Davies
DIRECTOR: Graeme Harper
STARS: David Tennant, Catherine Tate, Bernard Cribbins, Billie Piper
ORIGINAL TRANSMISSION: 6/21/2008

An alien fortune teller transports Donna back to a pivotal moment in her life, prompting her to make a different choice and change time forever. This is a powerful science-fiction variant of *It's a Wonderful Life*, depicting a nightmarish reality in which an everyday decision by a seemingly unimportant individual results in one earth-shattering tragedy after another. Piper returns as an older, more world-weary Rose, but it's once again Tate who steals the show with her multi-layered performance.

A. According to the Doctor, the Time Beetle which attaches itself to Donna's back is in the employ of what recurring villain from *The Sarah Jane Adventures*?

B. In the alternate timeline, which of the Doctor's former companions perishes alongside Martha Jones when the Royal Hope Hospital is transported to the moon?

C. Guest star Clive Standen reprises his role of Private Harris, first introduced in what earlier Tenth Doctor tale?

D. Chipo Chung, who portrays the sinister fortune teller here, previously appeared in "Utopia/The Sound of Drums/Last of the Time Lords" in what role?

E. The members of Torchwood are presumed killed while combating what invading aliens in the alternate reality?

"The Stolen Earth/Journey's End"

WRITER: Russell T. Davies
DIRECTOR: Graeme Harper
STARS: David Tennant, Catherine Tate, Billie Piper, Freema Agyeman, Elisabeth Sladen, John Barrowman, Noel Clarke, Eve Myles, Camille Coduri, Gareth David-Lloyd, Tommy Knight, John Leeson, Bernard Cribbins, Alexander Armstrong
ORIGINAL TRANSMISSION: 6/28-7/5/2008

A slam-bang free-for-all featuring the Daleks, Davros, most of the Tenth Doctor's companions and friends, U.N.I.T., and a host of major players from *Torchwood* and *The Sarah Jane Adventures*. The Daleks snatch planets from every corner of time and space in order to construct a massive bomb that can destroy reality itself. Though it treads dangerously close to overkill with so many characters, plot threads, and wild contrivances, this all-star reunion delivers too much pulse-pounding action and heart-tugging emotion to be anything but a rip-roaring, edge-of-your-seat triumph.

A. What former British official contacts the Doctor's friends and former companions via the sub-wave communications network?

B. Martha uses what experimental teleportation device, salvaged from the earlier conflict with the Sontarans, to escape U.N.I.T. headquarters during the Dalek invasion?

C. What real-life evolutionary scientist, who is married to former companion actress Lalla Ward, appears as himself in this story?

D. The Doctor and Donna visit the headquarters of what galactic law enforcement agency to inquire about the missing planets?

E. Julian Bleach, who portrays the insidious Davros here, appears as what eponymous villain in the Fourth Season opener of *The Sarah Jane Adventures*?

"The Next Doctor"

WRITER: Russell T. Davies
DIRECTOR: Andy Goddard
STARS: David Tennant, David Morrissey, Velile Tshabalala
ORIGINAL TRANSMISSION: 12/25/2008

The Doctor meets a man claiming to be a future incarnation of the Time Lord in nineteenth-century London. The new Cybermen make a triumphant return in this highly entertaining, extremely well-acted holiday effort. The scene in which the Tenth Doctor reveals the terrible truth about Morrissey's character is a real tearjerker, and Dervla Kirwan chews the snowy scenery with aplomb as the vengeful villainess, Miss Hartigan.

A. According to the man claiming to be the next Doctor, the acronym TARDIS stands for what?

B. Before directing this story, Andy Goddard helmed several episodes of *Torchwood*, including what 2006 outing about an alien fight club in Wales?

C. Guest star Michael Bertenshaw went on to appear in three episodes of the 2009 mini-series *Murderland*, alongside what former cast member of *The Sarah Jane Adventures*?

D. What are the furry Cyborg servants of the Cybermen called?

E. Who do the Cybermen forcibly recruit to construct the CyberKing?

"Planet of the Dead"

WRITERS: Russell T. Davies, Gareth Roberts
DIRECTOR: James Strong
STARS: David Tennant, Michelle Ryan
ORIGINAL TRANSMISSION: 4/11/2009

In this funny, frothy adventure, the Doctor, a comely cat burglar, and a group of bewildered bus passengers are transported to a distant planet populated by metallic stingrays and humanoid flies. Comedian Lee Evans is a bit over the top as a bumbling U.N.I.T. scientist assisting the Doctor from Earth, but the curvaceous Ryan, the scenic Dubai locations, and the state-of-the-art special effects make this one a sexy, sumptuous visual feast.

A. Michelle Ryan played the title role in what short-lived 2007 revival of a popular 1970s science-fiction spin-off series?

B. The Doctor and Christina (Michelle Ryan) encounter what humanoid insects in the desert?

C. Guest star Adam James appeared in a 2008 episode of *Secret Diary of a Call Girl*, a dramatic series starring what former *Doctor Who* companion actress?

D. Guest star Ellen Thomas appeared with David Morrissey, star of "The Next Doctor," in what universally panned 2006 big-screen sequel?

E. U.N.I.T. Captain Erisa Magambo (Noma Dumezweni) first appeared in what earlier Tenth Doctor story?

"The Wedding of Sarah Jane Smith"

(The Sarah Jane Adventures)

WRITER: Gareth Roberts
DIRECTOR: Joss Agnew
STARS: Elisabeth Sladen, David Tennant, Tommy Knight, Daniel Anthony, Anjli Mohindra, John Leeson, Alexander Armstrong
ORIGINAL TRANSMISSION: 10/29-10/30/2009

The Doctor intervenes when his former companion walks down the aisle with a man who is not at all what he seems. Tennant has some excellent interplay with Anthony and the rest of the youthful cast, but Sladen rules the day with perhaps the strongest, most moving performance of her lengthy career. This one will have fans of both series hoping for a rematch between the Time Lord and the treacherous Trickster.

A. Sarah Jane jokingly asks if she should send the Doctor's invitation to her wedding to what planet?

B. The slug-like alien that emerges from a parcel is native to what planet?

C. Paul Marc Davis, who plays the Trickster, previously appeared as the Chieftain of the savage Futurekind in what *Doctor Who* story?

D. Brigadier Lethbridge-Stewart can't attend Sarah Jane's wedding because he's once again on assignment in what South American country?

E. Producer Nikki Smith went on to produce what later *Doctor Who* special?

"The Waters of Mars"

WRITERS: Russell T. Davies, Phil Ford
DIRECTOR: Graeme Harper
STARS: David Tennant, Lindsay Duncan
ORIGINAL TRANSMISSION: 11/15/2009

A classic *Doctor Who* plot is turned on its ear as the Doctor must decide if being the last of the Time Lords gives him the right to rewrite history by saving the crew of a doomed Mars expedition from aquatic monsters. What begins as an exceptionally creepy but straightforward horror tale turns into a riveting morality play as the darkest, most self-indulgent aspects of Tennant's characterization take over. The shocking final scene will haunt even the most jaded viewer long after the closing credits roll.

A. The Doctor lands on Mars on what historic date?

B. As a child, Adelaide Brooks was inspired to become an astronaut by the sight of what alien creature?

C. Which member of the Bowie Base One crew is the first to be infected by the virus?

D. The first of Alan Ruscoe's many guest appearances in *Doctor Who* came in what 2005 episode?

E. The Doctor is visited by what familiar alien being at the end of this episode?

"The End of Time"

WRITERS: Russell T. Davies, Steven Moffat
DIRECTOR: Euros Lynn
STARS: David Tennant, Bernard Cribbins, Catherine Tate
ORIGINAL TRANSMISSION: 12/25/2009-1/1/2010

The resurrected Master uses alien technology to rewrite the DNA of every human on Earth on the eve of the vengeful return of the Time Lords. The Davies era comes to a spectacular close with this rather illogical but wholly unforgettable epic. Though the script plays fast and loose with continuity and reveals little about the all-important Time War itself, the players are given one amazing, emotionally charged scene after another, and they all rise to the occasion. Lesser actors might have mishandled the Master's animalistic mania or the Doctor's overt self-pity, but John Simm and the departing Tennant deliver performances for the ages. Cribbins' redemptive, *Star Wars*-inspired tail gunner scene is a guaranteed crowd-pleaser.

A. Alexandra Moen, who plays Lucy Saxon, appeared alongside former *Doctor Who* star Paul McGann and former guest star

Kathryn Drysdale in what 2006 six-part British/Australian co-production?

B. The device dubbed the "Immortality Gate" by Joshua Naismith (David Harewood) is actually a piece of medical equipment belonging to what alien race?

C. The Doctor addresses the Lord High President of Gallifrey (Timothy Dalton) by what legendary name?

D. Which two former companions are revealed to have become husband and wife since we last saw them?

E. What acclaimed Scottish actor provides the voice of the Elder Ood, who warns the Doctor of the Master's return from the dead?

(Answers begin on Page 247.)

The Eleventh Doctor

2009-Present

WHEN MATT SMITH STEPPED INTO THE ROLE OF THE Doctor, he faced the same challenges as Peter Davison had in the early 1980s — being the youngest actor ever to play the iconic alien, and replacing an immensely popular leading man who redefined the character forever. Like Davison, Smith quickly proved himself equal to the task.

The athletic Smith turned to acting when a serious back injury curtailed his professional football aspirations. After several critically acclaimed turns on the stage, he found small-screen success alongside former *Doctor Who* companion actress Billie Piper in the television adaptations of Philip Pullman's *The Ruby in the Smoke* and *The Shadow in the North*.

The Eleventh Doctor is slightly more reserved and detached than his previous regeneration, but no less unpredictable. He often seems to be reasoning something complex and completely unrelated out in his mind even as he's carrying on a heated discussion with the person standing in front of him. He displays an acute eye for detail, a fondness for children, and a visible discomfort when he finds himself the object of romantic attraction. This Doctor guards his emotions much more closely than his last two selves did.

The Eleventh Doctor continues to travel in the TARDIS, saving the universe from destruction on an almost daily basis.

"The Eleventh Hour"

WRITER: Steven Moffat
DIRECTOR: Adam Smith
STARS: Matt Smith, Karen Gillan, Arthur Darvill, Caitlin Blackwood
ORIGINAL TRANSMISSION: 4/3/2010

In the strongest regeneration story since the 1970s, the Doctor has twenty minutes to stop aliens from incinerating the Earth to destroy an escaped intergalactic prisoner. First-time actress Blackwood is excellent as young Amelia Pond, but it's the instant chemistry between the brilliantly off-kilter Smith and the fetching, feisty Gillan that makes this story unforgettable. The scene in which the Eleventh Doctor is formally introduced to the alien Atraxi is guaranteed to make longtime fans giddy with glee.

A. What object from her childhood does the Doctor give to Amy (Karen Gillan) to prove he's traveled through time?

B. What odd breakfast finally satisfies the Doctor's cravings following his regeneration?

C. Caitlin Blackwood is the real-life cousin of what regular *Doctor Who* cast member, who she had never met in person until working on the series?

D. Guest star Tom Hopper also appeared in a 2010 episode of what BBC fantasy series, based on a legendary wizard who, according to the Seventh Doctor serial "Battlefield," may actually have been the Doctor?

E. What real-life astronomer and self-made celebrity appears as himself in this episode?

"The Beast Below"

WRITER: Steven Moffat
DIRECTOR: Andrew Gunn
STARS: Matt Smith, Karen Gillan
ORIGINAL TRANSMISSION: 4/10/2010

The Doctor and Amy must uncover the sinister secret of *Starship UK*, where the citizens regularly vote to have their own memories erased rather than face the truth about their past. Reminiscent of 1980s stories like "Vengeance on Varos" and "The Happiness Patrol," this atmospheric, twenty-ninth-century tale is loaded with continuity references to both old and new series alike. Smith and Gillan really shine in the closing moments, when the Doctor's relationship to his strong-willed new companion is put to a major test.

A. Why isn't the Doctor allowed to vote?

B. Amy investigates a hole in the ship in front of a Magpie Electricals shop, a business first seen in what Tenth Doctor story?

C. In the TARDIS, the Doctor receives a telephone call from what historical figure?

D. Before guest starring in this episode, Terrence Hardiman appeared in an episode of what short-lived 1990s comedy series about a time-traveling TV repairman?

E. Guest star Hannah Sharp appears in what 2010 dramatic film with "Blink" star Carey Mulligan?

"Victory of the Daleks"

WRITER: Mark Gatiss
DIRECTOR: Andrew Gunn
STARS: Matt Smith, Karen Gillan
ORIGINAL TRANSMISSION: 4/17/2010

Shades of "Power of the Daleks" as the Doctor and Amy discover that Winston Churchill and his top research scientist have developed lethal new machines to defeat the Nazis — machines that look and sound just like Daleks. The new series' second visit to World War II-era London is a visual feast, replete with *Star Wars*-style space battles involving Spitfires and colorful, redesigned Daleks, but also a showcase for guest actors Ian McNeice and Bill Paterson. McNeice is spot-on as Churchill, while Paterson's Professor Bracewell is a touching and tragic figure.

A. What is the name of the girl for whom Bracewell harbors a secret crush?

B. Before learning the truth, Bracewell and Churchill refer to the Daleks as what?

C. What does "KBO" stand for?

D. Ian McNeice briefly reprises his role as Churchill in what later Eleventh Doctor story?

E. Guest star Colin Prockter appears as a chef in what Ninth Doctor story?

"The Time of Angels/Flesh and Stone"

WRITER: Steven Moffat
DIRECTOR: Adam Smith
STARS: Matt Smith, Karen Gillan, Alex Kingston
ORIGINAL TRANSMISSION: 4/24-5/1/2010

The Doctor and Amy are recruited by the mysterious River Song to capture an escaped Weeping Angel, but soon discover they are trapped in a cavern full of the stone monsters. The long-awaited return of Moffat's alien Angels is wonderfully creepy and suspenseful, while the sharp interplay between Smith, Gillan, and the delightful Kingston provides some tension-breaking levity. As effective as it all is, however, the primary narrative is somewhat overshadowed by a racy coda in which Moffat puts to bed the notion of a Doctor-companion romance forever.

A. The Weeping Angel causes the crash of what interstellar vessel?

B. Prior to appearing in *Doctor Who*, guest star Iain Glen played a ruthless scientist in two of the *Resident Evil* films, as well as the power-hungry villain of what 2001 film based on another popular video game franchise?

C. River Song inscribes what words in Old High Gallifreyan text on the doomed ship's Home Box?

D. What uncredited actress who plays one of the Weeping Angels also appears in Tim Burton's 2010 3-D film *Alice in Wonderland*?

E. Amy is scheduled to marry Rory (Arthur Darvill) on what date?

"The Vampires of Venice"

WRITER: Toby Whithouse
DIRECTOR: Jonny Campbell
STARS: Matt Smith, Karen Gillan, Arthur Darvill
ORIGINAL TRANSMISSION: 5/8/2010

The Doctor takes Amy and her fiancé, Rory, to sixteenth-century Venice, where they discover that bloodsucking aliens are invading via the city's famous canals. This underrated tale is great fun, beginning with a hilarious encounter at a modern-day stag party and culminating in a tense confrontation between the Time Lord and the villainous Signora Rosanna Calvieri (Helen McCrory). Fast pacing and fine performances (particularly from Darvill) keep this admittedly formulaic adventure from floundering.

A. Guest star Helen McCrory plays what rather reluctant villainess in the last three *Harry Potter* films?

B. The alien vampires are from what planet?

C. The Doctor flashes a library card featuring a photo of which of his previous incarnations?

D. What British actress and model plays the blonde vampire girl who menaces the Doctor and his companions?

E. What do Rory and the Doctor hear as they enter the TARDIS to depart from Venice?

"Amy's Choice"

WRITER: Simon Nye
DIRECTOR: Catherine Morshead
STARS: Matt Smith, Karen Gillan, Arthur Darvill
ORIGINAL TRANSMISSION: 5/15/2010

Though saddled with perhaps the worst title in *Doctor Who* history, this nightmarish romp proves a fine showcase for the excellent performances of Gillan, Darvill, and guest villain Toby Jones. The Doctor and his companions shift back and forth between two equally deadly realities, and must decide which is a dream and which is real before it's too late to save themselves. The final revelation about the Dream Lord's true nature will have longtime fans wondering if they've actually seen the character before, in the guise of a certain Gallifreyan prosecutor from one of the original series' most controversial stories.

A. The powerless TARDIS is being pulled toward what cosmic body?

B. Guest star Nick Hobbs previously played what Peladonian character in two Third Doctor serials?

C. The elderly citizens of Leadworth are actually what type of aliens?

D. Guest star Audrey Ardington appears in what story from the first season of *The Sarah Jane Adventures*?

E. The Leadworth Rory makes what cosmetic decision to demonstrate his love for Amy?

"The Hungry Earth/Cold Blood"

WRITER: Chris Chibnall
DIRECTOR: Ashley Way
STARS: Matt Smith, Karen Gillan, Arthur Darvill
ORIGINAL TRANSMISSION: 5/22-5/29/2010

The Silurians return, bringing with them the classic *Doctor Who* plot structure and plenty of Third Doctor-era thrills. An experimental drilling operation in twenty-first-century Wales arouses the ire of a tribe of subterranean reptile men, who capture Amy and prepare for war with the surface-dwelling humans. Smith's moving scenes with a frightened little boy (Samuel Davies) and a shocking final twist involving the recurring crack in time and space are highlights of this satisfying throwback adventure.

A. Who do Amy and Rory see standing in the distance shortly after their arrival in Wales?

B. The Silurians were last seen in what Fifth Doctor serial?

C. What does Rory ask Amy not to wear outside of the TARDIS?

D. Neve McIntosh, who plays the Silurian warrior Alaya, appears in what 2010 BBC drama with Tenth Doctor actor David Tennant?

E. What two types of produce does the Doctor ask the Silurians for after they finish experimenting on him?

"Vincent and the Doctor"

WRITER: Richard Curtis
DIRECTOR: Jonny Campbell
STARS: Matt Smith, Karen Gillan
ORIGINAL TRANSMISSION: 6/5/2010

The Doctor and Amy must save Vincent Van Gogh from an invisible alien monster that torments him. For profoundly moving moments, this bittersweet episode is second to none. Tony Curran delivers a truly magnificent performance as the eccentric, temperamental Van Gogh, while Bill Nighy is excellent as a modern museum curator who worships the ill-fated artist. Gillan does her finest work of the season in the closing moments, when Amy comes to the heartbreaking realization that some tragedies cannot be averted. Without question, the finest historical story of the new series to date.

A. What do Amy and the Doctor see in Van Gogh's painting *The Church at Auvers* that shouldn't be there?

B. Bill Nighy played what monstrous villain in the films *Pirates of the Caribbean: Dead Man's Chest* and *Pirates of the Caribbean: At World's End*?

C. Richard Curtis is the only writer to have worked on every episode of the long-running *Blackadder* television series, which starred what "alternative" Ninth Doctor actor?

D. To thank her for inspiring him, Van Gogh leaves a personal inscription for Amy on which of his famous paintings?

E. The Doctor tells Van Gogh that he has also met Renaissance painter Michelangelo and what twentieth-century Cubist?

"The Lodger"

WRITER: Gareth Roberts
DIRECTOR: Catherine Morshead
STARS: Matt Smith, Karen Gillan
ORIGINAL TRANSMISSION: 6/12/2010

The Doctor unknowingly plays the role of romantic rival in this light, funny sci-fi take on traditional sitcoms, in which the Time Lord moves into a London flat to investigate a mysterious alien force upstairs. James Corden and Daisy Haggard are quite amiable as best friends too timid to take their relationship to the next level, but it is the contrast between Smith's off-beat, fish-out-of-water alien and the conventions of everyday contemporary Earth life that give this tale its considerable charm.

A. In addition to his work on *Doctor Who*, Gareth Roberts co-wrote the pilot episode of what spin-off series?

B. Craig has a postcard advertising an art exhibit featuring the works of what painter stuck to his refrigerator door?

C. What forgotten object does Amy find while rummaging through the Doctor's jacket pocket?

D. James Corden appeared with Eight Doctor actor Paul McGann in what 2008 horror comedy?

E. Before displaying his prowess as a footballer here, the Doctor demonstrated his cricket skills in what 1982 serial?

"The Pandorica Opens/The Big Bang"

WRITER: Steven Moffat
DIRECTOR: Toby Haynes
STARS: Matt Smith, Karen Gillan, Arthur Darvill, Alex Kingston
ORIGINAL TRANSMISSION: 6/19-6/26/2010

The Doctor, Amy, and River Song are lured to ancient Stonehenge, where they learn the terrible truth about the legendary Pandorica and face off against an army of the Time Lord's deadliest enemies. From the opening cameos by the season's high-profile guest stars to the joyful closing scene and ominous teaser of things to come, this funny, action-packed adventure is perfect in almost every way. An epic, emotional two-parter wholly deserving of a place among the very best *Doctor Who* stories of all time.

A. In what Seventh Doctor serial is the Time Lord shown wearing a fez and holding a mop?

B. River Song poses as what historical figure to gain access to the Roman encampment?

C. What alien sentry do the Doctor and Amy find in the chamber beneath Stonehenge?

D. Guest star Sophie Okonedo previously appeared as Liz Ten in what story?

E. Unable to use his TARDIS, the Doctor uses what device to jump around in time?

"Death of the Doctor" *(The Sarah Jane Adventures)*

WRITER: Russell T. Davies
DIRECTOR: Ashley Way
STARS: Elisabeth Sladen, Matt Smith, Daniel Anthony, Anjli Mohindra, Katy Manning
ORIGINAL TRANSMISSION: 10/25-10/26/2010

The Doctor's second foray outside of his own series is a rousing love letter to the Time Lord's past assistants from former *Doctor Who* executive producer Russell T. Davies. Skeptical ex-companions Sarah Jane Smith and Jo Jones attend the funeral of the Doctor, whose body has reportedly been brought to Earth by the buzzard-like Shansheeth. Great villains, a delightfully scatterbrained performance by Manning, a warm and wistful reunion between Jo and the Doctor, and plenty of references to other beloved ex-companions make this a thoroughly crowd-pleasing nostalgia trip.

A. How many of the Doctor's regenerations had Jo met prior to encountering the Eleventh Doctor in this story?

B. Why can't former companion Liz Shaw attend the Doctor's funeral?

C. Guest star Laila Rouass was a regular in the third season of what ITV science-fiction series about dinosaurs transported through time to contemporary Earth?

D. What guest star shares the same common last name with his on-screen character?

E. According to the Doctor, how many times can he change his physical appearance?

"A Christmas Carol"

WRITER: Steven Moffat
DIRECTOR: Toby Haynes
STARS: Matt Smith, Karen Gillan, Arthur Darvill
ORIGINAL TRANSMISSION: 12/25/2010

Steven Moffat has a knack for presenting inherently silly story elements in a way that makes them seem entirely organic and credible, and that gift has never been more evident than in his first holiday special. The Doctor must reform a callous old miser who holds the key to saving the lives of Amy, Rory, and thousands of passengers on an out-of-control starship on Christmas Eve. A clever script and excellent performances by Smith and guest star Michael Gambon make this relatively low-key reworking of Charles Dickens' classic a winner.

A. Abigail Pettigrew is played by what world famous mezzo-soprano vocalist?

B. What is the entry code number for Kazran Sardick's cryogenic storage facility?

C. What regular cast member's name appears in the opening titles for the first time in this episode?

D. During his many Christmas Eve adventures with Abigail and the young Kazran, the Doctor accidentally gets engaged to what American sex symbol of the 1950s and early '60s?

E. For their honeymoon, Amy is dressed in her Kiss-O-Gram police uniform, while Rory has donned what historical garb?

(Answers begin on Page 254.)

Answer Key

"An Unearthly Child"

A. *Day of the Triffids.*
B. The assassination of U.S. President John F. Kennedy.
C. 76 Totter's Lane.
D. John Smith and the Common Men.
E. Horg (Howard Lang).

"The Daleks"

A. Twenty-one.
B. "Planet of the Daleks" and "Genesis of the Daleks."
C. Static electricity.
D. *A Clockwork Orange.*
E. Episode Four ("The Ambush").

"The Edge of Destruction"

A. Quinnis.
B. Eight.
C. Ian (William Russell).
D. A faulty spring.
E. A giant footprint.

"Marco Polo"

A. The TARDIS.
B. Backgammon.
C. "The Wedding of Sarah Jane Smith." (It's unusual because it's a two-part tale from the spin-off *The Sarah Jane Adventures*, the first time the Doctor appears in a canonical televised story outside of his own series.)
D. Tegana (Derren Nesbitt).
E. *Coronation Street.*

"The Keys of Marinus"

A. De3O2.
B. "Silver Nemesis."
C. Five.
D. The human body.
E. George Coulouris.

"The Aztecs"

A. Cameca (Margot Van der Burgh).
B. Yetaxa.
C. The Perfect Victim.
D. "The Colony in Space."
E. *The Feathered Serpent.*

"The Sensorites"

A. Esto.
B. One.
C. Molybdenum.
D. Jacqueline Hill.
E. *Doomwatch.*

"The Reign of Terror"

A. England.
B. Regional Officer of the Provinces.
C. "The War Games."
D. "An Unearthly Child."
E. Napoleon Bonaparte (Tony Wall).

"Planet of Giants"

A. DN6.
B. *Dad's Army*.
C. The doors open in mid-flight.
D. A dead earthworm.
E. Dudley Simpson.

"The Dalek Invasion of Earth"

A. Are You Being Served?
B. The Slyther (Nick Evans).
C. The waters of the Thames River.
D. Hannibal.
E. "The Five Doctors."

"The Rescue"

A. Sydney Wilson.
B. Barely a hundred.
C. Earth.
D. A flare pistol.
E. 550 years old.

"The Romans"

A. Maximus Pettulian (Bart Allison).
B. 10,000 sesterces.
C. *Carry On*.
D. Peter Diamond.
E. They accidentally set fire to Nero's architectural plans, inspiring the Emperor to burn the city.

"The Web Planet"

A. Rosalyn de Winter.
B. Atmosphere Density Jackets.
C. Gold.
D. As cattle.
E. "Bad Wolf/The Parting of the Ways."

"The Crusade"

A. "The Daleks' Master Plan" and "Battlefield."
B. The Third.
C. Sir Ian of Jaffa.
D. *For Your Eyes Only*.
E. The Fifth (by the impostor King John, in "The King's Demons") and the Tenth (by Queen Victoria, in "Tooth and Claw").

"The Space Museum"

A. Revolution.
B. An empty Dalek casing.
C. "The Sontaran Experiment."
D. Boba Fett.
E. The Daleks.

"The Chase"

A. "The Chase."
B. A robot duplicate of the Doctor.
C. The Beatles.
D. The Sagaro Desert.
E. *Frankenstein Created Woman* (1967).

"The Time Meddler"

A. Stonehenge.
B. The Battle of Hastings.
C. "An Unearthly Child."
D. Ronald Rich.
E. "Dimension" was changed to the plural "Dimensions."

"Galaxy 4"

A. Chumblies.
B. Stephanie Bidmead.
C. School teacher.
D. Ammonia.
E. "The Pandorica Opens/The Big Bang."

"Mission to the Unknown"

A. Varga plants.
B. William Hartnell.
C. Verity Lambert.
D. They begin transforming into Vargas.
E. "Marco Polo" and "The Massacre of St. Bartholomew's Eve."

"The Myth Makers"

A. Cressida.
B. Ivor Salter.
C. Zeus.
D. *The Mind of the Enemy*.
E. Ten years.

"The Daleks' Master Plan"

A. Adam Mitchell, who joined the Doctor and Rose in "Dalek" but was expelled from the TARDIS after attempting to bring future technology to twenty-first-century Earth in "The Long Game."
B. Nicholas Courtney
C. The Monk (Peter Butterworth).
D. "The Invasion."
E. Spar.

"The Massacre of St. Bartholomew's Eve"

A. Dorothea.
B. The Abbot of Amboise.
C. Male.
D. Two years.
E. 1966.

"The Ark"

A. Gerry Davis.
B. Richard Beale.
C. 700 years.
D. Whipsnade Zoo.
E. "The End of the World."

"The Celestial Toymaker"

A. Hopscotch, on an electrified floor.
B. 1023.
C. Sergeant Rugg (Campbell Singer).
D. "Arc of Infinity."
E. The Ice Warriors.

"The Gunfighters"

A. Lynda Baron.
B. Individual episode titles.
C. A giant tooth.
D. Doctor Caligari.
E. $1,000.

"The Savages"

A. "The Traveler from Beyond Time."
B. Chal (Patrick Godfrey) and Tor (Ewen Solon).
C. "Planet of Evil."
D. A jewel-studded mirror.
E. *Downtime.*

"The War Machines"

A. Will Operating Thought ANalogue.
B. Post Office Tower.
C. Doctor Who.
D. Twelve.
E. Kenneth Kendall.

"The Smugglers"

A. Lowest UK TV ratings (4.5 million viewers).
B. Cherub (George A. Cooper).
C. A dislocated finger.
D. A metal spike.
E. "The Trade-Ins."

"The Tenth Planet"

A. Voyagers!
B. The Z Bomb.
C. Zeus 4.
D. Radiation.
E. Three.

"The Power of the Daleks"

A. In a mercury swamp.
B. Cyril Luckham.
C. Three.
D. Edward Kelsey.
E. Bragen (Bernard Archard).

"The Highlanders"

A. Donald McCrimmon.
B. Brian Hayles.
C. Doktor van Wer.
D. The *Annabelle*.
E. *Robin Hood*.

"The Underwater Menace"

A. "The Time Monster."
B. Episode Three.
C. Ramo (Tom Watson).
D. By draining the oceans into the Earth's core.
E. "The Celestial Toymaker."

"The Moonbase"

A. The Gravitron.
B. "Horror of Fang Rock" and "Full Circle."
C. Doctor Evans (Alan Rowe).
D. "Faint Hearts."
E. The food storage room.

"The Macra Terror"

A. The Doctor's face.
B. Polly's screams.
C. Sandra Bryant and Karol Keyes (Luan Peters).
D. The Danger Gang.
E. *The Abominable Dr. Phibes* (1971) and *Dr. Phibes Rises Again* (1972).

"The Faceless Ones"

A. "Time and the Rani."
B. Chameleon Tours.
C. Gatwick Airport.
D. Pauline Collins.
E. It's stolen.

"The Evil of the Daleks"

A. 144.
B. Ice Warriors.
C. Turning base metals to gold.
D. Alpha, Beta, and Omega.
E. "Turn Left."

"The Tomb of the Cybermen"

A. About 450 years old.
B. *Twins of Evil.*
C. Cybermats.
D. The Brotherhood of Logicians.
E. Producer Peter Bryant.

"The Abominable Snowmen"

A. The Ghanta (a bell).
B. Deborah Watling.
C. *The Abominable Snowman* (1957).
D. "Twinkle, Twinkle, Little Star."
E. A real Yeti.

"The Ice Warriors"

A. The Ioniser.
B. "The Waters of Mars."
C. "The Resurrectionists."
D. A Sonic Cannon.
E. A computer.

"The Enemy of the World"

A. By watching a televised speech.
B. Sydney Newman.
C. "The Invasion of Time."
D. Assistant to his personal chef.
E. *Moonbase 3*.

"The Web of Fear"

A. Colonel.
B. Tina Packer.
C. Sergeant Benton.
D. A glass pyramid.
E. A miniature Yeti model.

"Fury from the Deep"

A. On the surface of the sea.
B. A heartbeat.
C. "The Idiot's Lantern."
D. The Sonic Screwdriver.
E. "The Moonbase."

"The Wheel in Space"

A. LX 88J.
B. Mark Strickson.
C. Parapsychology Librarian.
D. Quick-set plastic.
E. John Smith.

"The Dominators"

A. Quarks.
B. "The Daleks' Master Plan."
C. 172 years.
D. Henry Lincoln (Henry Soskin).
E. "The Eleventh Hour."

"The Mind Robber"

A. Romana (Mary Tamm, Lalla Ward), K-9 (John Leeson, David Brierly), and Kamelion (Gerald Flood, Dallas Adams, Anthony Ainley).
B. The Anti-Molecular Ray Disintegrator.
C. "The Time Monster" and "The Horns of Nimon."
D. *Out of the Unknown*.
E. "The Deadly Assassin."

"The Invasion"

A. International Electromatics.
B. *She-Wolf of London*.
C. Planet 14.
D. "Remembrance of the Daleks."
E. Episode Three.

"The Krotons"

A. Tellurium.
B. Eighteen.
C. The Dynatrope.
D. James Cairncross.
E. *UFO*.

"The Seeds of Death"

A. Professor Eldred's Rocketry Museum.
B. Izlyr ("The Curse of Peladon") and Azaxyr ("The Monster of Peladon").
C. One.
D. *The Omen*.
E. Episode Four.

"The Space Pirates"

A. Eighteen.
B. *The Invisible Man.*
C. The LIZ-79.
D. Peter Bryant.
E. *Moon Zero Two.*

"The War Games"

A. A fog-like force field.
B. Michael Craze.
C. "The Wheel in Space."
D. SIDRATs.
E. The Quarks ("The Dominators").

"Spearhead from Space"

A. Cambridge.
B. "The Keeper of Traken."
C. A cobra tattoo.
D. 1000 million years.
E. The Spidron.

"Doctor Who and the Silurians"

A. WHO 1.
B. The Moon.
C. "Voyage of the Damned."
D. *Blake's 7.*
E. The Van Allen radiation belt.

"The Ambassadors of Death"

A. Sergeant Benton.
B. The Time Vortex Generator.
C. Davros.
D. The Space Security Department.
E. Peter Halliday.

"Inferno"

A. Dracula.
B. Venusian karate.
C. The Republican Security Forces (RSF).
D. "The Talons of Weng-Chiang."
E. Fire extinguishers.

"Terror of the Autons"

A. Captain Mike Yates (Richard Franklin).
B. The National Space Museum.
C. "The Seeds of Death."
D. Colonel Masters.
E. A telephone cord.

"The Mind of Evil"

A. Roger Delgado.
B. Koquillion ("The Rescue").
C. The Thunderbolt missile.
D. *The Empire Strikes Back.*
E. Don Houghton.

"The Claws of Axos"

A. The Director General.
B. The Nuton Power Complex.
C. A second-hand gas stove.
D. "The Masque of Mandragora."
E. K-9.

"The Colony in Space"

A. Uxarieus.
B. The Crab Nebula.
C. *The Master.*
D. The Interplanetary Mining Corporation (IMC).
E. "Enlightenment."

"The Daemons"

A. 60,000 light years.
B. Mr. Magister.
C. "Utopia/The Sound of Drums/The Last of the Time Lords."
D. Barry Letts and Robert Sloman.
E. OLR 461 E.

"Day of the Daleks"

A. Sir Reginald Styles (Wilfred Carter).
B. *General Hospital* (1972-1979).
C. The Blinovitch Limitation Effect.
D. The Master.
E. "Image of the Fendahl."

"The Curse of Peladon"

A. Aggedor.
B. Stuart Fell (body) and Ysanne Churchman (voice).
C. Temmosus.
D. Trisilicate.
E. "Midnight."

"The Sea Devils"

A. Eocenes.
B. *A Matter of WHO.*
C. Jabba the Hutt.
D. HMS *Seaspite.*
E. *Clangers* (1969-1974).

"The Mutants"

A. 3000 Earth years.
B. *The Savages.*
C. "The Brain of Morbius."
D. Ky (Garrick Hagon).
E. *Quatermass and the Pit* (aka *Five Million Miles to Earth*).

"The Time Monster"

A. "Warriors of the Deep."
B. Transmission of Matter through Interstitial Time.
C. *Horror of Frankenstein* (1970) and *Frankenstein and the Monster from Hell* (1974).
D. Sergeant Benton.
E. A Chronovore.

"The Three Doctors"

A. Frances Pidgeon.
B. The Dematerialization Circuit.
C. "The War Games."
D. His recorder.
E. Antimatter.

"Carnival of Monsters"

A. A Miniscope.
B. *The Two of Us.*
C. 1926.
D. John Sullivan.
E. "Business trip."

"Frontier in Space"

A. Dragons.
B. Roger Delgado.
C. Karol Keyes.
D. Sirius 4.
E. *The War of the Worlds.*

"Planet of the Daleks"

A. "Genesis of the Daleks."
B. Plant sap.
C. The Plain of Stones.
D. *Foyle's War.*
E. Ice.

"The Green Death"

A. The Nuthutch.
B. Metebelis 3.
C. *1984*.
D. *Freewheelers*.
E. Bimorphic Organisational Systems Supervisor.

"The Time Warrior"

A. Gallifrey.
B. *Time Bandits*.
C. Lavinia.
D. "Horror of Fang Rock."
E. An Osmic Projector.

"Invasion of the Dinosaurs"

A. WV0 2M.
B. A Tyrannosaurus Rex.
C. James Marcus.
D. "The Celestial Toymaker."
E. Operation Golden Age.

"Death to the Daleks"

A. Psychokinesis.
B. Parrinium.
C. *The Quatermass Experiment*.
D. *Survivors*.
E. A Peruvian temple.

"The Monster of Peladon"

A. Rima.
B. Ice Warriors.
C. Galaxy 5.
D. "Horror of Fang Rock."
E. Alpha Centauri.

"Planet of the Spiders"

A. "The Final Game," by Robert Sloman.
B. "Ghost Light."
C. A blue crystal from Metebelis 3.
D. *Village of the Damned.*
E. A Time Lord.

"Robot"

A. J.P. Kettlewell (Edward Burnham).
B. "Planet of the Spiders."
C. Patricia Maynard.
D. The Alpha Centaurian Table Tennis Club.
E. "Frontier in Space."

"The Ark in Space"

A. Madame Nostradamus.
B. "The Sanctuary."
C. A yo-yo.
D. Lazar.
E. *Farscape.*

"The Sontaran Experiment"

A. Tom Baker.
B. Via transmat beam.
C. Kevin Lindsay.
D. The Terullian Diode Bypass Transformer.
E. "Enemy of the Bane."

"Genesis of the Daleks"

A. "Invasion of the Dinosaurs."
B. A Time Ring.
C. Lieutenant Malcolm Reed (Dominic Keating).
D. Davros.
E. The Mark III Travel Machine.

"Revenge of the Cybermen"

A. Pluto-Earth Flight 15.
B. Neophobas.
C. The glitter gun.
D. "The Mind Robber."
E. Wookey Hole Caves.

"Terror of the Zygons"

A. "Timelash."
B. "The Power of the Daleks."
C. The Scottish Energy Commission.
D. Lieutenant Harry Sullivan.
E. Nicholas Courtney.

"Planet of Evil"

A. *The Tempest.*
B. *Romeo and Juliet* and *Hamlet.*
C. Morestra.
D. "Blink."
E. Vishinsky (Ewen Solon).

"The Pyramids of Mars"

A. 1980.
B. Lewis Greifer.
C. 740.
D. A respiratory bypass system.
E. "The Deadly Assassin."

"The Android Invasion"

A. Ginger beer.
B. Mother.
C. A scarf.
D. Geneva.
E. "The Highlanders."

"The Brain of Morbius"

A. His severed arm.
B. "The Talons of Weng-Chiang."
C. The Elixir of Life.
D. Cyanogen.
E. Terrance Dicks and Robert Holmes.

"The Seeds of Doom"

A. The World Ecology Bureau.
B. Hubert Rees.
C. Major Beresford (John Acheson).
D. *Lexx*.
E. The Galactic Flora Society.

"The Masque of Mandragora"

A. A captain in Cleopatra's guard.
B. *Quantum of Solace* (2008).
C. *Hamlet, Prince of Denmark*.
D. "The End of the World."
E. The Brethren of Demnos.

"The Hand of Fear"

A. Kastria.
B. Judith Paris and Stephen Thorne.
C. "The Awakening."
D. *Daddy Wouldn't Buy Me a Bow Wow*.
E. *K-9 and Company*.

"The Deadly Assassin"

A. Borusa.
B. "The End of Time."
C. Four (Angus MacKay, John Arnott, Leonard Sachs, Philip Latham).
D. Tersurus.
E. "The Massacre of St. Bartholomew's Eve."

"The Face of Evil"

A. Janis thorns.
B. *The Star Wars Holiday Special* (1978).
C. The Test of the Horda.
D. *C.A.T.S. Eyes.*
E. William Tell.

"The Robots of Death"

A. Grimwade's Syndrome.
B. *Never Say Never Again.*
C. D84 (Gregory de Polnay).
D. Chub (Rob Edwards).
E. Cotton.

"The Talons of Weng-Chiang"

A. 5000.
B. *Star Trek.*
C. Zygma energy.
D. Giant rats.
E. "Invasion of the Dinosaurs."

"The Horror of Fang Rock"

A. Ruta 3.
B. *Thriller.*
C. *Flannan Isles.*
D. Diamonds.
E. Blue.

"The Invisible Enemy"

A. 3922.
B. Professor Marius (Frederick Jaeger).
C. Six ("The Ark," "The Mind of Evil," "Pyramids of Mars," "The Invisible Enemy," "Castrovalva," and "Remembrance of the Daleks").
D. Ten minutes.
E. *Are You Being Served?*

"Image of the Fendahl"

A. Benedict Cumberbatch.
B. Salt.
C. Kenya.
D. "Nightmare of Eden.'
E. A pentagram.

"The Sun Makers"

A. 5000 talmars.
B. Public steaming.
C. *Night of the Demon* (aka *Curse of the Demon*).
D. Henry Woolf.
E. Mars.

"Underworld"

A. The P7E.
B. Diana Dors.
C. "The quest is the quest!"
D. *The Omega Factor*.
E. The Time Lords.

"The Invasion of Time"

A. "The Deadly Assassin."
B. Graham Williams and Anthony Read.
C. Hilary Ryan.
D. A Demat Gun.
E. K-9 Mark II.

"The Ribos Operation"

A. Romanadvoratrelundar.
B. 759 years old.
C. Jethrik.
D. *Super Gran*.
E. *Trog*.

"The Pirate Planet"

A. 523 years.
B. Zanak.
C. *Inseminoid.*
D. "Army of Ghosts/Doomsday."
E. Isaac Newton.

"The Stones of Blood"

A. The Great Seal of Diplos.
B. "Guardian of the Abyss."
C. The Tau Ceti system.
D. John Aubrey.
E. *The Adventures of Sir Lancelot.*

"The Androids of Tara"

A. A dragon-shaped segment of a statue, on the Gracht estate.
B. "The Macra Terror."
C. Fishing.
D. The King's scepter.
E. *A for Andromeda.*

"The Power of Kroll"

A. Philip Madoc.
B. Swampies.
C. *Chocky.*
D. Seven.
E. Weapons.

"The Armageddon Factor"

A. Theta Sigma.
B. Gandalf.
C. *The Haunting.*
D. Chronodyne.
E. 008 01 0040.

"Destiny of the Daleks"

A. *The Origins of the Universe* by Oolon Caluphid.
B. Arcturus.
C. A Randomiser.
D. "Dragonfire."
E. *MacGyver.*

"City of Death"

A. 125 years old.
B. John Cleese.
C. *Hamlet.*
D. *Jupiter Moon.*
E. "This is a fake."

"The Creature from the Pit"

A. Tythonus.
B. Terry Walsh.
C. Morris Barry.
D. Metal.
E. 74,384,338.

"Nightmare of Eden"

A. 900.
B. Peter Purves.
C. Vraxoin.
D. Galactic Salvage Insurance.
E. Irongron.

"The Horns of Nimon"

A. Crinoth.
B. Paint his ship white.
C. *Blue Peter.*
D. Jacenite.
E. Graham Crowden.

"The Leisure Hive"

A. Twenty minutes.
B. The Tachyon Recreation Generator.
C. Question marks.
D. *Devil Girl from Mars.*
E. Lalla Ward.

"Meglos"

A. Zolfa-Thura.
B. Ti.
C. Freema Agyeman and Karen Gillan.
D. Gallifrey.
E. The Martians.

"Full Circle"

A. *The Awakening*.
B. A Badge of Mathematical Excellence.
C. A CVE (Charged Vacuum Emboitment).
D. Terradon.
E. *The Curse of the Fly*.

"State of Decay"

A. The Time Lords.
B. Seventeen.
C. A Sontaran.
D. The *Hydrax*.
E. "Terror of the Vervoids."

"Warriors' Gate"

A. "You were the noblest Romana of them all."
B. *X the Unknown.*
C. Tom Baker.
D. Human slaves.
E. Gundans.

"The Keeper of Traken"

A. The Master's TARDIS.
B. "Timelash."
C. Tremas.
D. Mettula Orionsis.
E. Cameca.

"Logopolis"

A. "The Time Monster."
B. A flat tire.
C. Adrian Gibbs.
D. Entropy.
E. "Charlie Boy."

"Castrovalva"

A. Twenty-five percent.
B. A celery stick.
C. Vicki and Jo.
D. "The Ambassadors of Death.'
E. Caroline John.

"Four to Doomsday"

A. The right.
B. "Enlightenment."
C. AA778.
D. Cato Fong.
E. *Principia Mathematica*.

"Kinda"

A. "Something Borrowed."
B. The Mara.
C. *Asylum*.
D. Ice cream.
E. The "Not We."

"The Visitation"

A. Michael Robbins.
B. The Sonic Screwdriver.
C. An android.
D. The Great Fire of London.
E. Peter Davison, whose real name is Peter Moffett.

"Black Orchid"

A. Ann Talbot.
B. The Orinoco.
C. "Ghost Light."
D. A screwdriver.
E. "Death in the Morning."

"Earthshock"

A. "Now I'll never know if I was right."
B. Music.
C. *The Nightmare Man.*
D. "Fragments."
E. Adric's Badge of Mathematical Excellence.

"Time-Flight"

A. Anthony Ainley.
B. He's wearing his Badge of Mathematical Excellence (which was destroyed in "Earthshock").
C. *The Lost Continent.*
D. Department C19.
E. Tegan.

"Arc of Infinity"

A. Borusa (Leonard Sachs).
B. John Nathan-Turner.
C. Leela.
D. "The Five Doctors."
E. *Sherlock Holmes and the Case of the Silk Stocking.*

"Snakedance"

A. The Scrampus system.
B. *Men Behaving Badly.*
C. Elisabeth Sladen.
D. 500 years.
E. "Time Crash/Voyage of the Damned."

"Mawdryn Undead"

A. Vorus.
B. Mathematics.
C. A rock.
D. "The Lottery Experiment."
E. 1979.

"Terminus"

A. Lazar's Disease.
B. Colin Baker.
C. Adric.
D. Hydromel.
E. Six.

"Enlightenment"

A. Ephemerals.
B. The *Buccaneer.*
C. *Voyage of the Damned.*
D. "The Crusade."
E. The celery stick on his lapel.

"The King's Demons"

A. Kamelion.
B. An iron maiden.
C. *Randall and Hopkirk (Deceased).*
D. In London.
E. Mark Bannerman.

"The Five Doctors"

A. "The Thirteenth Reunion."
B. The Black Scrolls of Rassilon.
C. A Raston Warrior Robot (Keith Hodiak).
D. A time eddy.
E. *The Satanic Rites of Dracula.*

"Warriors of the Deep"

A. 2084.
B. The Myrka.
C. *The House that Dripped Blood.*
D. *Star Cops.*
E. Sentinel 6.

"The Awakening"

A. Her grandfather, Andrew Verney (Frederick Hall).
B. The Queen of the May.
C. The Terileptils.
D. "Image of the Fendahl."
E. Kamelion (Gerald Flood).

"Frontios"

A. Jeff Rawle.
B. An acid battery.
C. "The Happiness Patrol."
D. Kolkokron.
E. The TARDIS hat stand.

"Resurrection of the Daleks"

A. Ninety years.
B. Leela and Kamelion.
C. The High Council of the Time Lords.
D. Rula Lenska.
E. *Unidentified Flying Oddball* (aka *The Spaceman and King Arthur*).

"Planet of Fire"

A. The United States of America.
B. Logar.
C. Lanzarote.
D. Sarah Jane Smith (Elisabeth Sladen), in "Death to the Daleks."
E. Kamelion.

"The Caves of Androzani"

A. Ten.
B. Bat's milk.
C. The Master.
D. *Julius Caesar.*
E. "Ghost Machine."

"The Twin Dilemma"

A. Azmael.
B. "Yuck!"
C. Interplanetary Pursuit, A Squadron.
D. Three.
E. Gavin and Andrew Conrad.

"Attack of the Cybermen"

A. The Chameleon Circuit.
B. Riften 5.
C. "The Tomb of the Cybermen."
D. Halley's Comet.
E. *The Day of the Triffids.*

"Vengeance on Varos"

A. Zeiton-7.
B. Jason Connery, son of Sean Connery.
C. The Galatron Mining Corporation.
D. "Genesis of the Daleks."
E. The Punishment Dome.

"The Mark of the Rani"

A. A cupboard.
B. Zoe Wanamaker.
C. "Stay Tuned."
D. George Stephenson (Gawn Grainger).
E. "Argue, mainly."

"The Two Doctors"

A. The Madillon Cluster.
B. *Frankenstein and the Monster from Hell.*
C. *Cleopatra.*
D. Kartz and Reimer.
E. Gumblejack.

"Timelash"

A. Morlox.
B. The Bandrils.
C. Mustakozene-80.
D. The Third Doctor.
E. "The Greatest Show in the Galaxy."

"Revelation of the Daleks"

A. "The City of Death."
B. Professor Arthur Stengos (Alec Linstead).
C. Bastic-headed bullets.
D. The Grand Order of Oberon.
E. "The Deadly Assassin."

"The Mysterious Planet"

A. Dominic Glynn.
B. RamJam FM.
C. An L3 maintenance robot.
D. A Black Light Generator.
E. *UK Habitats of the Canadian Goose* by "H.M. Stationery Office."

"Mindwarp"

A. A Sontaran.
B. The Mentors.
C. Martha Jones.
D. The Tronkonp Empire.
E. *Aliens*.

"Terror of the Vervoids"

A. Carrot juice.
B. *The Avengers*.
C. The *Hyperion 3*.
D. *Captain Nemo and the Underwater City*.
E. *K-9 and Company*.

"The Ultimate Foe"

A. "Ten million years of absolute power."
B. "The Twin Dilemma."
C. The Key of Rassilon.
D. "The War Games."
E. Paul McCartney.

"Time and the Rani"

A. Mel.
B. 953 years old.
C. "The Keys of Marinus."
D. C.P. Snow.
E. "Children of Auron."

"Paradise Towers"

A. Kroagnon.
B. "The Tomb of the Cybermen."
C. The Rezzies.
D. On the roof.
E. *Those Fantastic Flying Fools* (aka *Jules Verne's Rocket on the Moon*).

"Delta and the Bannermen"

A. Shangri-La.
B. His question mark umbrella.
C. *FairyTale: A True Story.*
D. "Survival."
E. They are the ten billionth customers to enter the Navarino spaceport.

"Dragonfire"

A. Dorothy.
B. Nation McKinley.
C. An Argolin.
D. Proamnon.
E. *Space Force.*

"Remembrance of the Daleks"

A. The Hand of Omega.
B. None. Fowler joined the series in 1959, the year after Hartnell's departure.
C. "The Robots of Death."
D. Roy Tromelly.
E. *The Fresh Prince of Bel-Air.*

"The Happiness Patrol"

A. Terra Alpha.
B. A Stigorax.
C. "As Time Goes By."
D. *A.D.A.M.*
E. *Rollerball.*

"Silver Nemesis"

A. "Dalek."
B. "Death Is But A Door."
C. *Fahrenheit 451.*
D. Arundel Castle.
E. Validium.

"The Greatest Show in the Galaxy"

A. Segonax.
B. "The Face of the Enemy."
C. *The Beast in the Cellar.*
D. The Gods of Ragnarok.
E. Singing squids.

"Battlefield"

A. Brigadier Winifred Bambera (Angela Bruce).
B. *Army of Darkness.*
C. "Earthshock."
D. "Planet of the Spiders."
E. Greyhound 1.

"Ghost Light"

A. The fang of a cave bear.
B. Kate O'Mara.
C. *Flash Gordon.*
D. "That's the Way to the Zoo."
E. 1983.

"The Curse of Fenric"

A. "I don't know."
B. Mrs. Birkett.
C. "Battlefield."
D. "Smith and Jones."
E. ULTIMA.

"Survival"

A. "Ghost Light."
B. "The Mysterious Planet."
C. Perivale.
D. Teleportation.
E. Song.

"Doctor Who: The Movie"

A. *$#*! My Dad Says.*
B. "Timelash."
C. A beryllium atomic clock.
D. *Frankenstein* (1931).
E. *My Bloody Valentine.*
F. Genghis Khan.
G. The Third ("Spearhead from Space") and the Eleventh ("The Eleventh Hour").
H. *The Lodger.*
I. A cold.
J. He's half human.

"Rose"

A. Article Fifteen of the Shadow Proclamation.
B. *The Second Coming.*
C. A wheelie bin.
D. Search-Wise.net.
E. *Hawks.*

"The End of the World"

A. Saliva.
B. "They Keep Killing Suzie."
C. Jiggery-pokery.
D. The Adherents of the Repeated Meme.
E. "State of Decay."

"The Unquiet Dead"

A. None.
B. Gwyneth.
C. Sneed and Company.
D. The Time War.
E. *A Christmas Carol.*

"Aliens of London/World War Three"

A. Raxacoricofallapatorius.
B. Dr. Toshiko Sato (Naoko Mori).
C. Flydale North.
D. 900 years old.
E. Lachele Carl (as American news reporter Trinity Wells).

"Dalek"

A. A Metaltron.
B. Rose.
C. *Stargate SG-1.*
D. Salt Lake City, UT.
E. *Ultraviolet.*

"The Long Game"

A. Floor 500.
B. Eva Saint Julienne.
C. 600.
D. *Journeyman.*
E. A Type Two Info-Spike Chip in his forehead.

"Father's Day"

A. *Survivors.*
B. November 7, 1987.
C. *Mansfield Park.*
D. "Don't Mug Yourself" by The Streets.
E. Reapers.

"The Empty Child/The Doctor Dances"

A. The Chula.
B. Albert Valentine.
C. Mrs. Harcourt (Vilma Hollingberry).
D. Nanogenes.
E. "The Sontaran Stratagem/The Poison Sky."

"Boom Town"

A. Bad Wolf.
B. "Remembrance of the Daleks."
C. *The Western Mail.*
D. Roald Dahl Plass.
E. Justicia.

"Bad Wolf/The Parting of the Ways"

A. *Big Brother.*
B. "Paradise Towers."
C. Jo Joyner.
D. A Delta Wave Generator.
E. Barcelona.

"Children in Need/The Christmas Invasion"

A. "Merry Christmas!"
B. *Ever Decreasing Circles.*
C. Blood control.
D. *Journey to the Center of the Earth.*
E. His hand is severed.

"New Earth"

A. The Face of Boe.
B. Chip.
C. "Gridlock."
D. All of them (every known disease).
E. Francine Jones, mother of Martha.

"Tooth and Claw"

A. James McCrimmon.
B. Ian Dury.
C. "The Faceless Ones."
D. John Simm.
E. The Torchwood Institute.

"School Reunion"

A. *Buffy the Vampire Slayer.*
B. The Skasis Paradigm.
C. Keira Knightley.
D. Science.
E. Aberdeen.

"The Girl in the Fireplace"

A. *Thunderbirds.*
B. Thirty-seven years old.
C. Tuberculosis.
D. *Being Human.*
E. An ion storm.

"Rise of the Cybermen/The Age of Steel"

A. Ricky.
B. David Tennant.
C. Zeppelins.
D. "Revelation of the Daleks."
E. A terrier.

"The Idiot's Lantern"

A. Elvis Presley.
B. Magpie Electricals.
C. "Small Worlds."
D. A Betamax videocassette.
E. *Truckers.*

"The Impossible Planet/The Satan Pit"

A. *Things to Do Before You're 30.*
B. Krop Tor.
C. Captain Walker.
D. *The Weakest Link.*
E. Jon Pertwee.

"Love and Monsters"

A. London Investigation 'N' Detective Agency.
B. (Harold) Saxon.
C. A Hoix (Paul Kasey).
D. "Double Jeopardy."
E. Clom.

"Fear Her"

A. Kelly Holmes.
B. An Isolus.
C. *Primeval.*
D. Huw Edwards.
E. *Casanova.*

"Army of Ghosts/Doomsday"

A. Freema Agyeman and Catherine Tate.
B. Residual void energy.
C. The Daleks and the Cybermen.
D. Bad Wolf Bay (Dårlig Ulv Stranden).
E. The Time Lords.

"The Runaway Bride"

A. In the TARDIS.
B. H.C. Clements.
C. "The End of Time."
D. The Tribophysical Waveform Macro-kinetic Extrapolator.
E. Howard Attfield.

"Smith and Jones"

A. A plasmavore.
B. A black X.
C. *Law & Order: UK.*
D. Röntgen radiation.
E. Kimmi Richards.

"The Shakespeare Code"

A. 1599.
B. *Harry Potter.*
C. "Author! Author!"
D. Global warming.
E. Donald Pleasence.

"Gridlock"

A. The Macra.
B. Bliss.
C. Ardal O'Hanlon.
D. Seven minutes.
E. "The End of the World."

"Daleks in Manhattan/Evolution of the Daleks"

A. *Dark Realm.*
B. New New York (on New Earth).
C. Dalek Sec.
D. *Star Wars Episode One: The Phantom Menace.*
E. "The Chase."

"The Lazarus Experiment"

A. Twelve hours.
B. Three (Mark Gatiss, Victor Pemberton, and Glyn Jones).
C. His dinner jacket.
D. *Color Me Kubrick.*
E. Southwark Cathedral.

"42"

A. The *S.S. Pentallian.*
B. They're married.
C. Elize du Toit.
D. The number of minutes until the *Pentallian* is destroyed.
E. *Running Wild.*

"Human Nature/The Family of Blood"

A. The Chameleon Arch.
B. A fob watch.
C. *A Journal of Impossible Things.*
D. *Spaced* (1999-2001).
E. Charles Dickens.

"Blink"

A. "The Mark of the Rani."
B. A key.
C. Transporting them back to the past and letting them live out their lives there.
D. 1969.
E. "The Daleks' Master Plan" and "The Dominators."

"Utopia / The Sound of Drums / Last of the Time Lords"

A. "You are not alone."
B. The Archangel Network.
C. *Moon Shot.*
D. Sharon Osbourne.
E. The Toclafane.

"Time Crash/Voyage of the Damned"

A. LINDA.
B. *Daleks–Invasion Earth 2150 A.D.*
C. "The Greatest Show in the Galaxy."
D. Jimmy Vee.
E. "The Stolen Earth/Journey's End."

"Partners in Crime"

A. Adipose Industries.
B. A mate.
C. It was "lost."
D. Billie Piper.
E. *Red Dwarf.*

"The Fires of Pompeii"

A. Karen Gillan.
B. The Pyrovile.
C. *Alien 3*.
D. A water pistol.
E. Paul McGann.

"Planet of the Ood"

A. 4126.
B. *The Simpsons*.
C. *The Young Indiana Jones Chronicles*.
D. Hair loss.
E. Harry Potter.

"The Sontaran Stratagem/The Poison Sky"

A. Torchwood.
B. The flying aircraft carrier *Valiant*.
C. Luke Rattigan (Ryan Sampson).
D. *Hellboy*.
E. *Jekyll*.

"The Doctor's Daughter"

A. Peter Davison.
B. David Tennant.
C. Messaline.
D. The Source.
E. Jenny.

"The Unicorn and the Wasp"

A. *The Good Life* (aka *Good Neighbors*).
B. A Vespiform.
C. Charlemagne.
D. "Inferno."
E. Mrs. Teresa Neele.

"Silence in the Library/Forest of the Dead"

A. *FlashForward.*
B. The Vashta Nerada.
C. Two.
D. *Inception.*
E. The Doctor.

"Midnight"

A. The Sapphire Waterfall.
B. Poosh.
C. Sky Silvestry (Lesley Sharp).
D. They aren't.
E. *Ghostboat.*

"Turn Left"

A. The Trickster.
B. Sarah Jane Smith.
C. "The Sontaran Stratagem/The Poison Sky."
D. Chantho.
E. The Sontarans.

"The Stolen Earth/Journey's End"

A. Harriet Jones (Penelope Wilton).
B. Project Indigo.
C. Richard Dawkins.
D. The Shadow Proclamation.
E. The Nightmare Man.

"The Next Doctor"

A. Tethered Aerial Release Developed in Style.
B. "Combat."
C. Yasmin Paige.
D. Cybershades.
E. Human children.

"Planet of the Dead"

A. *Bionic Woman.*
B. The Tritovores.
C. Billie Piper.
D. *Basic Instinct 2.*
E. "Turn Left."

"The Wedding of Sarah Jane Smith"

A. Metebelis 3.
B. Polongus.
C. "Utopia/The Sound of Drums/Last of the Time Lords."
D. Peru.
E. "The Waters of Mars."

"The Waters of Mars"

A. November 21, 2059.
B. A Dalek.
C. Andy Stone (Alan Ruscoe).
D. "Rose" (as an Auton).
E. Ood Sigma (Paul Kasey).

"The End of Time"

A. *Tripping Over.*
B. The Vinvocci.
C. Rassilon.
D. Mickey Smith and Martha Jones.
E. Brian Cox.

"The Eleventh Hour"

A. An apple with a face carved in it.
B. Fish fingers and custard.
C. Karen Gillan.
D. *Merlin.*
E. Patrick Moore.

"The Beast Below"

A. He's neither human nor a British subject.
B. "The Idiot's Lantern."
C. Winston Churchill.
D. *Goodnight Sweetheart.*
E. *Never Let Me Go.*

"Victory of the Daleks"

A. Dorabella.
B. Ironsides.
C. Keep buggering on.
D. "The Pandorica Opens/The Big Bang."
E. "The Long Game."

"The Time of Angels/Flesh and Stone"

A. The *Byzantium.*
B. *Lara Croft: Tomb Raider.*
C. "Hello, sweetie!"
D. Caroline Royce.
E. June 26, 2010.

"The Vampires of Venice"

A. Narcissa Malfoy.
B. Saturnyne.
C. The First Doctor (William Hartnell).
D. Gabriella Wilde.
E. Silence.

"Amy's Choice"

A. A cold star.
B. Aggedor.
C. The Eknodine.
D. "Eye of the Gorgon."
E. He cuts off his ponytail.

"The Hungry Earth/Cold Blood"

A. Themselves.
B. "Warriors of the Deep."
C. Her engagement ring.
D. *Single Father.*
E. Celery and tomatoes.

"Vincent and the Doctor"

A. The face of a monster.
B. Davy Jones.
C. Rowan Atkinson, who played the Doctor in the comedic special, "The Curse of Fatal Death."
D. *Vase with 12 Sunflowers.*
E. Pablo Picasso.

"The Lodger"

A. *The Sarah Jane Adventures.*
B. Vincent Van Gogh.
C. Her engagement ring.
D. *Lesbian Vampire Killers.*
E. "Black Orchid."

"The Pandorica Opens/The Big Bang"

A. "Silver Nemesis."
B. Cleopatra.
C. A Cyberman.
D. "The Beast Below."
E. A Vortex Manipulator.

"Death of the Doctor"

A. Three.
B. She is on the U.N.I.T. base on the moon.
C. *Primeval.*
D. Finn Jones (playing Jo's grandson, Santiago).
E. 507.

"A Christmas Carol"

A. Katherine Jenkins.
B. 7258.
C. Arthur Darvill.
D. Marilyn Monroe.
E. A Roman Centurion costume.

Index of Story Titles

Bear Manor Media

Classic Cinema.
Timeless TV.
Retro Radio.

WWW.BEARMANORMEDIA.COM

www.ingramcontent.com/pod-product-compliance
Lightning Source LLC
Chambersburg PA
CBHW061722270326
41928CB00011B/2081
9781593936372